The Mustard Seed Process

The Mustard Seed Process

Twelve Practical Exercises on
Social Justice
for Groups and Individuals

Helen Swift, S.N.D. deN.
and
Frank Oppenheim, S.J.

Paulist Press
New York/Mahwah

Acknowledgment:

The publisher gratefully acknowledges use of the excerpt from the book *LIFEFORCE: The Psycho-Historical Recovery of the Self* by Jean Houston. Copyright © 1980 by Jean Houston. Reprinted by permission of Delacorte Press.

Library of Congress
Catalog Card Number: 85-62878

ISBN: 0-8091-2759-8

Published by Paulist Press
997 Macarthur Boulevard
Mahwah, N.J. 07430

Printed and bound in the United States of America

Our deep appreciation is due to

Margaret Telscher, S.N.D. deN.
Margaret Roalef
Cecile Rench
Peggy Feltrup Becker
Marilyn Kaiser
Marcia Sichol, S.H.C.J.
Adelaide L. Wessling
and
Joseph Bracken

*for reading the manuscript
and
giving many valuable suggestions*

Introduction

Within the past decade, numerous books have been written about justice, often from the Latin American perspective. The ordinary Christian may well question what has been happening to bring about this emphasis on justice. Justice has always been a Christian virtue but since the Synod of Bishops in 1971 new understandings have highlighted the place of justice in the life of a Christian.

The most quoted passage of *Justice in the World,* the document coming from that Synod of Bishops, makes it clear that there is an integral relationship between justice and faith. The bishops stated, "Action on behalf of justice and participation in the transformation of the world fully appear to us as a constitutive dimension of the preaching of the Gospel, or, in other words, of the Church's mission for the redemption of the human race and its liberation from every oppressive situation."

In making this very strong statement closely linking action for justice to the mission of the Church, the bishops were responding to the signs of the times. There have always been people in need and, from the time of Jesus, the Church has always responded by feeding the poor, nursing the sick, educating the ignorant—in a word, carrying on the works of mercy. Done in the name of Jesus all these works of charity filled the presently urgent needs of individuals.

Today our world is much more complicated. People

1

are no longer needy only because of unfortunate circumstances or perhaps natural disasters. In our industrial, technological world, masses of people, even whole nations are oppressed and deprived of their rights because of the unjust structures of society. These structures include the customary attitudes of one culture versus another, laws, trade agreements, regulations, and certain ways of doing things—all of which keep some groups in poverty and work to the advantage of others. Works of charity can alleviate only the results of these unjust structures. They do not change the structures. It takes works of justice to get to the roots of the oppression, to change the structures and liberate the oppressed. The bishops are saying that the Church, all of us as the people of God, must work for the human race's "liberation from every oppressive situation." Just as it is our faith that makes us the people of God, so it is our faith that calls us to works of justice.

Our faith, although it includes a belief in a creed or a system of tenets, is much more than that. It involves a total submission of intellect and will to all that God has revealed. As we read God's revelation in the Gospels, it is obvious that Jesus favored the poor, sinners, the blind, the deaf, the marginal people of his day. Today these are the people who are suffering oppression from unjust structures. These are the people who need our help to be liberated from oppression.

This book presents various types of encounters with justice issues. It gives you the opportunity to bring your faith face to face with these situations and meet the challenge to respond. The key, then, to using this book effectively is participation. In each chapter you will meet two or three people. Some of them you will meet for the first time; others may be old friends. Through your interaction with these people you will be led to reflect on some of your own values, to get in touch with your feelings and to evaluate some aspects of your life. You will also be given the opportunity to test your feelings and reactions through experiments. Rather than a book you read straight through, this one is like a recipe book, to be used bit by bit, each page intended to stimulate your experience and reflection.

This book invites you into a process; it moves gradually from some reflections on your own attitudes and values, through a consideration of fairness in inter-personal relationships, to facing some of the broader justice issues. The whole process is meant to be something you experience. The value of the experience for you will depend on how deeply you, as an individual, enter into the process.

Although you can use this book individually, you can greatly enrich your experience by sharing your reflections, thoughts and insights with a small group. An ideal size group for such sharing is eight to twelve members. Here are a few practical steps you might take to facilitate the group moving smoothly into the process:

1. At the organizational meeting, settle practical details such as frequency of meeting, location, a definite time for opening and closing the meeting. The time limits for the meeting are important. People then realize they are there for a purpose; they are not at a social gathering.
2. Decide on a leader for your group. One person may take this responsibility or you may wish to rotate the leadership role. In either case, the leader for a particular meeting is responsible for the tone of the meeting. The contributions of each person need to be received reverently. No one should be pressured to speak but each should be given an opportunity to gift the others. Differences of opinion can be enriching for the group or they can lead to a heated debate. If each member of the group has an open mind, realizing that no one has the total truth but everyone has some truth, then each can be enriched by the

others. The leader needs to be alert to the receptivity of the group and watch for signs of an argumentative spirit.

3. Spend some time together at the organizational meeting looking at the various sections of Chapter 1. Each of the chapters has the following sections:

(a) An introduction to the theme of the chapter through a case for your reflection.

(b) An experiment to help you get in touch with your own attitudes and feelings on the subject.

(c) An incident in the life of Jesus which exemplifies the values centered in the theme.

(d) Some thoughts which expand and develop the subject.

(e) The example of a contemporary person who has incorporated the values in his or her life.

Each of these first five sections is followed by questions for your personal reflection and discussion in the group.

(f) A call to take another small step to grow in practicing justice more wholly.

Make sure that each member understands the process. Your goal for the next meeting is to read and reflect on each section. As you reflect during the week, jot down your insights, your thoughts, your feelings—anything you want to share with the group. Your notes will help you remember what you want to share with the group when you next meet. They may be especially enlightening to you if you review them at the end of the program.

4. There is one word of caution that needs to be added about the sharing. There are things in one's life that are too personal to share. You may find some of the questions for reflection very personal and be tempted to skip them because you would not feel you could share your thoughts and feelings with the group. It is important for a group beginning a program such as this to realize that

not every insight is meant to be shared. Some of your insights may be meant *only* for you.

Those who work for justice, trying to change unjust structures, find that it is very difficult, if not impossible, to do alone. One needs the encouragement and support of a faith community. When you encounter in faith the insights and values of other Christians you will begin to experience a sense of community. You will find that, through your sessions together, you will be gifting one another with new understandings and insights. Through respectful discussion and clarifying comments everyone has an opportunity to grow in faith and Christian commitment. In this way your time together will also be "faith encounters."

The importance of a faith foundation in working for justice is highlighted by the Council fathers: "This faith needs to prove its fruitfulness by penetrating the believer's entire life, including its wordly dimensions, and by activating him toward justice and love, especially regarding the needy" (*The Church Today,* #21). Faith, then, is the activating principle of justice, but to be truly Christian, justice must be motivated by love and be an expression of love. Through this link to love, justice becomes part of living out God's basic commandment to love one's neighbor as oneself. Just as justice must be motivated by love, true love must be expressed fairly. The purpose of this book is to assist *you* in giving an honest answer to the question, "Are you loving fairly?"

1. Carol

Carol is a young mother with three small children, ages five, three and one. She wants to raise her children to be good Christians, to have happy, productive lives. Carol has a good marriage, lives in a middle-class neighborhood and has a number of congenial friends. As she looks at her life, she feels she should be happy but she finds that most of the time she is depressed.

Carol worries about her children, afraid that something might happen to one of them. Her oldest daughter, Sarah, has just started kindergarten. Carol has instructed her well about not talking to strangers and never getting into a car alone with anyone but her father. Still Carol cannot relax until she sees the school bus stop at the corner and Sarah come running up the street.

She has given up reading the newspaper or watching any TV newscasts because she feels overwhelmed by all the terrible things that are happening in the world. There is so much violence, hunger, oppression, unemployment, predictions of economic troubles, besides all kinds of natural disasters in various parts of the world. Any mention of nuclear weapons fills her with panic as she thinks of the dangers to her beautiful children.

Carol's husband, Jim, tries to cheer her up by telling her that she is not responsible for the misfortunes of the world. Everything is so complicated that no one knows the solutions to the problems. Even the experts disagree on the best course to take. He says, "There is no use worrying, Carol. Somehow things will work out."

Carol felt she had to watch the TV show "The Day After" since it received so much publicity and she knew all her friends would be talking about it. She did not want to admit to anyone that any talk of nuclear war made her anxious and depressed. She had trouble sleeping for several nights after viewing the show. She went into the children's room often during the night and just gazed at them sleeping so peacefully. She just knew that they would never have a chance to grow up.

Questions for Your Reflection

1. Compare Carol's and Jim's views of the world. Does either one have any hope for the future? If so, on what is that hope based?

2. Is the world view of either Carol or Jim realistic? Explain.

3. Do you believe that conditions in the world are getting worse all the time? Give evidence for your answer.

4. State briefly your own world view at this time.

An Experiment

Suppose there is a very powerful microscope that can reveal you to yourself. Take a look through that microscope now.

1. What do you find in your life at present that gives you hope?

2. How would you complete the sentence, "Life is . . ."?

3. Do you find any traces of the Holy Spirit in your life now?

4. What evidence do you see that the Holy Spirit was present and active in your life in the past?

Now focus the microscope on the world.
5. What do you find there that gives you hope?
6. What indications do you find that the Spirit is present and active in the world today?

GOSPEL EVENT

"Filled with the Holy Spirit, Jesus left the Jordan and was led by the Spirit through the wilderness, being tempted there by the devil for forty days. During that time he ate nothing, and at the end he was hungry. Then the devil said to him, 'If you are the Son of God, tell this stone to turn into a loaf.' But Jesus replied, 'Scripture says, "Man does not live on bread alone."'

"Then leading him to a height, the devil showed him in a moment of time all the kingdoms of the world and said to him, 'I will give you all this power and the glory of these kingdoms; for it has been committed to me and I give it to anyone I choose. Worship me, then, and it shall all be yours.' But Jesus answered him, 'Scripture says, "You must worship the Lord your God; and serve him alone."'

"Then he led him to Jerusalem and made him stand on the parapet of the temple. 'If you are the Son of God,' he said to him, 'throw yourself down from here, for Scripture says: "He will put his angels in charge of you to guard you," and again: "They will hold you up on their hands in case you hurt your foot against a stone."' But Jesus answered him, 'It has been said: "You must not put the Lord your God to the test."' Having exhausted all these ways of tempting him, the devil left him, to return at the appointed time" (Luke 4:1–13).

The evangelists tell us in the form of three temptations how Jesus learned more fully what it meant for him to announce the kingdom. These temptations might more appropriately be called testings. There were many options

9

open to Jesus, many different ways he might have announced to the people that the reign of God had come. Through the power of the Spirit within him he recognized that some of those options did not reflect the goodness and love of God. He was not to draw people to the Father through showering them with material things, through manipulating them with power, or through dazzling them with spectacular displays.

Jesus understood that he was not to take the easy way. He was challenged to accept with a courageous heart his role of Suffering Servant described by the prophet Isaiah. Jesus knew that he was risking rejection, hostility and even death by countering the popular beliefs of the Jews about the Messiah. After this desert experience "Jesus returned in the power of the Spirit to Galilee, and his reputation spread throughout the region" (Luke 4:14).

Very shortly after his return to Galilee Jesus went to his home in Nazareth and revealed to his friends and relatives what he had learned in the desert about his mission.

"He came to Nazareth, where he had been brought up, and went into the synagogue on the sabbath day as he usually did. He stood up to read, and they handed him the scroll of the prophet Isaiah. Unrolling the scroll he found the place where it was written: 'The Spirit of the Lord has been given to me, for he has anointed me. He has sent me to bring the good news to the poor, to proclaim liberty to captives, and to the blind new sight, to set the downtrodden free, to proclaim the Lord's year of favor.' He then rolled up the scroll, gave it back to the assistant and sat down. And all eyes in the synagogue were fixed on him. Then he began to speak to them, 'This text is being fulfilled today even as you listen.' And he won the approval of all, and they were astonished by the gracious words that came from his lips" (Luke 4:16–22).

Questions for Your Reflection

1. Read the first Scripture passage again slowly, trying to be very present to Jesus as together you are led into the desert. How do you feel about going into the desert? How do you think Jesus felt as he faced his public life?

2. How did Jesus respond to the challenges of the devil?

3. As a result of these testings, how did Jesus come to view the public life he was just beginning?

4. What have you learned from the testings and challenges you have faced in your life?

5. What are your attitudes toward justice as you begin this program of reflection and action?

6. There was a surge of hope and expectation in the people as Jesus announced, "This text is being fulfilled today." How do you feel when you hear that the mission of Jesus fulfills the prophecy of Isaiah?

7. What do you believe is the relationship of Christians today to the mission of Jesus?

8. In what ways can you participate in the mission of Jesus?

A WORD OF CHRISTIAN WITNESS

Psychologists point out that each person has a basic vision of life that colors one's thoughts, that influences behavior and enters into all relationships. The vision of life may be either conscious, that is, one is aware of it and can articulate it, or it may be unconscious. In either case, it is operating in the individual's behavior.

As you begin this series of reflections on justice it is well to come to grips with your own basic orientation to life. Like Carol, one may say, "Life is threatening," and see danger everywhere. All one's energies then become focused on taking pre-cautions, installing alarms, imagining every possible danger so one is prepared to counteract it. Life becomes a constant search for greater and greater security. At the same time this person becomes more and more convinced that one's best efforts are not going to be enough.

Jim, Carol's husband, tries to reassure his wife, but his basic orientation to life is very passive too. He might say, "Life is a problem," or "Life is a puzzle with lots of missing pieces." However, there is a glimmer of hope in Jim's vision. He does have the feeling that "somehow things will work out," someone will find those missing pieces. But Jim doesn't make a move to do his part, however small it might be, to find those missing pieces.

We have an entirely different picture of Jesus as he came out of the baptismal waters and strode purposefully into the desert. Jesus recognized that the kingdom was at hand and he allowed himself to be led by the Spirit into the desert to further clarify his mission.

To appreciate the full impact of Jesus' message we would have to be very familiar with the context of the passage he quoted from Isaiah. For Isaiah was encouraging the people of his time by telling them that the Messiah would bring comfort to those in sorrow, he would take away their listless spirit, he would relieve them of oppression and want. Life would be very different for all the "little" people, for all those distressed in any way. Their lives would be so changed that "they will be called oaks of justice planted by the Lord to show his glory" (Isaiah 61:3). In a word, in God's kingdom there would be justice and peace for even the most lowly. Now Jesus is saying that the moment has arrived, that God's reign is now.

Luke goes on to tell us the reaction of Jesus' friends to this statement. At that moment they had the wonderful opportunity of lifting their lives above the petty concerns of Nazareth and being actively involved in the greatest adventure of all time. Unfortunately, their joy and enthusiasm faded and they turned aside when it became evident that the kingdom did not meet their expectations. They were not ready for a kingdom reached by faith, humble service and following Jesus with his cross.

As Jesus moved through his public life, Spirit-filled and Spirit-led, he was always faithful to the mission he had received from his Father. He proclaimed the good news to the poor, he healed lepers, paralytics, demoniacs, the blind, the deaf, he fed the hungry, raised the dead, gave peace and forgiveness to sinners. Each incident was a way of saying, "See, the kingdom is really here; God's Spirit is at work in his world."

After two thousand years, there are still starving people in Africa, oppressed people in Central America, the elderly poor in our city slums, those who are discriminated against because of color, race or sex. There are wars, conflicts among nations and in families, people suffering from injustices of every kind.

But something else has not changed either. There is still the opportunity to take part in the struggle against injustice. It *is* an opportunity to give life greater meaning, to do something worthwhile by making a contribution to the justice and peace of the world. That would be a scary thought if we had to rely on our own courage and strength. But we are not alone, for we have one another, and our puny human efforts are given life and power by the Spirit of Jesus.

On the night before he died, Jesus promised his disciples that they too would be filled with the Spirit so they could carry on his work of spreading the kingdom. On the very evening of his resurrection, in his first appearance to them he said, "Receive the Holy Spirit" (John 20:22).

Again, fifty days later, there was a dramatic outpouring of the Spirit, a visible sign that the Spirit of Jesus was at work in the infant Church. Through baptism we are inserted into the life and death of Jesus; we too receive his Spirit. Because of the Spirit within us, we are able to take on the values of Jesus and to reflect those values by the way we live. This transformation through the Spirit does not happen all at once. It is an ongoing, lifelong process.

By reflecting on what happened at Pentecost we can understand what effect the Spirit should have on us. The disciples of Jesus were frightened, uncertain, unsure of what they should do now that Jesus was no longer in their midst in the way they were accustomed to finding him. As they were all gathered on the day of Pentecost there were two signs that they were being touched by God. The powerful wind that filled the whole house revealed to the waiting disciples the activity of God. They knew of the many times in their Jewish history when God manifested himself as wind, or, as they said, "the breath of God." From that first moment of creation, God's breath was always life-giving, invigorating, and energizing. They felt ready to throw open the doors and rush out to tell of the wonders of the Lord.

The Spirit within us is life-giving too. Trusting in the Spirit, we feel a confidence to do what of ourselves we could not do. We can look at our mixed-up world and believe that in spite of appearances to the contrary, there is a way out of the complicated problems. When we are tempted to sink into depression and apathy as we see the overwhelming numbers of people who are hungry, oppressed, tortured and even assassinated, the Spirit is within to give us new life if we but ask. We need never depend on our weak human abilities to confront the injustice of the world, for we have the power and energy of the Spirit to rely on.

The second sign of God's outpouring of the Spirit on Pentecost was the tongues of fire that settled on each of the disciples. They were aflame with a burning enthusiasm for God and his word. They could no longer hide the faith that was in them; they had to go out and share it with others. They found that language barriers were broken down in their hearers and they were able to communicate with people of many different backgrounds. They experienced in an intensified way what happens whenever, through the power of the Spirit, there is open communication and faith-sharing.

The Spirit wants to lead us too to the openness with one another that leads to community. As you read and reflect on the justice issues presented in this book you may feel your own inadequacy to change unjust structures or even to make any significant changes in your own life. However, if you share your reflections and concerns with other Spirit-led persons, you may find a bond of community growing in the group. You may experience support and strength as together you allow the Spirit to lead you to growth in justice.

Questions for Your Reflection

1. Why is it so important to be in touch with your feelings as you begin this program?
2. Do you look upon working for justice as an opportunity? Why or why not?
3. Where do you find courage to meet the challenges of your life?
4. Have you experienced the presence of the Spirit helping you to communicate more fully in truth?

A TWENTIETH CENTURY WITNESS

When Tom Dooley studied at St. Louis University Medical School his professors predicted that he was des-

15

tined to become a "society doctor." Little did they know then how he would meet the challenge of the suffering refugees of Vietnam. As a young naval doctor in 1954 he was aboard the ship that began transporting refugees from the Tonkin Delta to South Vietnam.

Two thousand refugees crowded aboard the transport ship that had been hastily changed from moving trucks and tanks to the simplest accommodations for the refugees. Dr. Dooley was faced with the gigantic task of treating tropical diseases he had never encountered in his studies. The people were covered with sores, many were starving and some had been mistreated and tortured by their enemies.

When the ship arrived at Haiphong, there were 150,000 refugees living in the most squalid conditions in the city streets. Dr. Dooley was assigned to set up the refugee camp there. His medical studies and his courses in philosophy and French had included nothing to prepare him for building a refugee camp. He began by having four hundred tents flown in from Japan and opened his camp on the outskirts of the city. The navy provided food and other bare essentials but did not deem it necessary to supply soap, vitamins or basic medicines. Dr. Dooley began writing to business firms in the United States describing the inhuman, unsanitary conditions of the camps. The response was so immediate and generous that Dr. Dooley was able to avoid any epidemics in the camps. The refugees had to be free from disease before they could be evacuated from the camp.

Commenting on this experience, Dr. Dooley remarked, "To me that experience was like the white light of revelation. It made me proud to be a doctor. Proud to be an American doctor who had been privileged to witness the enormous possibilities of medical aid in all its Christlike power and simplicity. Was that why the foreign aid planners, with their billion-dollar projects, found it diffi-

cult to understand?" (*Dr. Tom Dooley's Three Great Books,*
Farrar, Straus and Cudahy, 1960, p. 133).

Several months after being released from the navy in
1956, Dr. Dooley was already planning to return to Southeast Asia to establish small privately financed medical
missions. Several years later when he discovered he had
cancer he established Medico to carry on his work in
Southeast Asia where he had opened clinics and hospitals
to minister to the people. After surgery, in spite of his ill
health, he returned to Southeast Asia and continued to
work untiringly until his death at the age of thirty-four.

One of the ways we can characterize the work of the
Spirit in our world today is to say that the Spirit, working
through people like Tom Dooley, engenders hope. We
sometimes feel that when all else fails, that is the time to
hope. However, it is more realistic to see hope as our basic
orientation toward the future. If we have hope we move
into the future with confidence. No matter how dark the
future looks, how massive the problems, we know that we
do not have to depend on our own inner resources. The
Spirit is within us and we are certain that there *is* a way
out.

In hope, we know that we do not have to solve *all* the
world's problems, but we do need to take that next step
into the future which makes our own limited world-space
a little more just. That first step might be changing some
of our attitudes toward justice.

Questions for Your Reflection

1. How was Tom Dooley able to accomplish so much
in such a short time?
2. Why is Tom Dooley such a symbol of hope even today, almost thirty years after his death?
3. Do you value this group experience enough that

you will come to it rather than go to a card game or a ball game?

4. Are you willing to make a commitment to this group to share your insights and experiences for the richer growth of all?

CALL TO ACTION

Dr. Tom Dooley gave everything—his talent, his energy, his health and his very life—to minister to people made destitute by war. What specific step will you take during the coming week to use your talent to help others?

2. *Madonna*

Madonna was the first in a family of five children. Madonna's mother seemed content caring for her husband, their five children and their large home. She took the responsibility for raising the children, teaching them Christian values and encouraging them to do their best. Madonna's father was reserved and hard-working, but very opinionated. He always knew best and nearly always had the last word. From early childhood Madonna learned not to cross him. As she grew up, her mother taught her all she needed to know to make a happy, peaceful home for her own future family.

Madonna married Bill, a young, handsome and very dynamic businessman, who was climbing rapidly in his advertising agency. Bill and Madonna loved each other, but their tastes and life-styles differed so greatly that Madonna began to think that it was more prudent to step aside for Bill rather than to confront him. Bill always respected Madonna and was courteous to her, but, like her father, he had definite ideas about the way the home should be run. He insisted that his newspaper always be ready beside his warm breakfast and that his evening dinner be on time when he returned from work. He was very particular about his appearance and expected Madonna to care for his clothing as though it were top priority in her family concerns. It was Madonna's duty too to draw up a monthly account of household expenses. He allowed her a generous budget for running the house but would not let her spend money on what he regarded as her indulgent artistic tastes.

After the day's hectic pace at the ad agency, Bill wanted peace and quiet in the evening. Madonna knew too how important an orderly, peaceful home was for the healthier rearing of their three children. There had been a few exchanges of angry words early in their marriage, but Madonna had soon learned that it promoted peace not to cross Bill. For the last dozen years she couldn't recall any real argument between herself and Bill. Going along with him made her angry at times but she told herself that in the long run it gave the children and Bill a better home atmosphere. She didn't think St. Paul was *completely* off base when he directed wives to be submissive to their husbands (Ephesians 5:21–23). She always included in her prayers a petition for "peace in our family."

Whenever Kim and Laura, her two girls, got into a childish fight, Madonna made them stop immediately or do without supper. If Billy, her youngest, returned home from play with torn pants, scratched arm or a black eye, Madonna insisted that he play peacefully with his companions or find new friends. She was determined that her children, especially the girls, learn the value of a peaceful home.

Questions for Your Reflection

1. What is Madonna's ideal of a happy family? Do you agree with her? Why or why not?
2. Will she develop her love for Bill by focusing only on his strengths? By always being submissive to him?
3. Does her commitment to "peace at any price" harm Bill, herself and her children? If so, in what ways?
4. Suppose Madonna decides to be more assertive in her relationship with Bill. What effect will this change

have on the family as a whole? on Madonna? on Bill? on the children?

An Experiment

1. Which of the following statements seem valid reasons for not getting involved in social problems?
2. Have you ever made any of these statements?
3. Rank these statements in order of the frequency which you have experienced them used by others.

Statements for Non-Involvement

a. I believe that if that's the way our government does things, it must be right.

b. I have my own problems; don't bother me.

c. I believe in keeping peace, not making waves.

d. I don't want to hurt my friends by taking a stand on any issues.

e. I have a right to all I can get; it's a dog-eat-dog world out there.

f. It burns me up to see my taxes used to help those lazy people on welfare. I worked hard for what I have; they can do the same.

g. I don't see any point in *doing* something; nothing changes anyway.

h. I don't like to admit it but the thought of nuclear war scares the hell out of me. I'm not sure what's the best solution to arms build-up, so I just stay out of it.

i. Life's too short—get what you can and enjoy it.

j. When I get upset about the mess in the world, I relax with a drink or two.

k. They'd better not come to me with all their problems. I'll tell them where they can go!

l. Everything's so complicated! I might just make matters worse by getting involved.

21

"The apostles rejoined Jesus and told him all they had done and taught. Then he said to them, 'You must come away to some lonely place all by yourselves and rest for a while'; for there were so many coming and going that the apostles had not time even to eat. So they went off in a boat to a lonely place where they could be by themselves. But people saw them going, and many could guess where; and from every town they all hurried to the place on foot and reached it before them. So as he stepped ashore he saw a large crowd; and he took pity on them because they were like sheep without a shepherd, and he set himself to teach them at some length. By now it was getting very late, and his disciples came up to him and said, 'This is a lonely place and it is getting very late, so send them away, and they can go to the farms and villages round about, to buy themselves something to eat.' He replied, 'Give them something to eat yourselves.' They answered, 'Are we to go and spend two hundred denarii on bread for them to eat?' 'How many loaves have you?' he asked. 'Go and see.' And when they had found out they said, 'Five and two fish.' Then he ordered them to get all the people together in groups on the green grass, and they sat down on the ground in squares of hundreds and fifties. Then he took the five loaves and the two fish, raised his eyes to heaven and said the blessing; then he broke the loaves and handed them to his disciples to distribute among the people. He also shared out the two fish among them all. They all ate as much as they wanted. They collected twelve basketfuls of scraps of bread and pieces of fish. Those who had eaten the loaves numbered five thousand men" (Mark 6:30–44).

Questions for Your Reflection

1. Put yourself in the place of Jesus as he gets off the boat and sees the crowd waiting for him. How do you feel and how would you react to having your day off ruined by people in need?
2. What significance do you see in Jesus getting the disciples involved in feeding the crowd?
3. Do you believe that Jesus is still concerned about the hungry and oppressed people of the world? If so, what is he doing about it? Give evidence for your answer.

A WORD OF CHRISTIAN WITNESS

Thus far in this chapter you have seen how Madonna and Jesus responded to unjust situations and have had the experience of testing some of your own responses. If one tends habitually to avoid confronting people, as Madonna did, one may need to look closely at Jesus in all aspects of his life. Many Christians have drawn from the Gospel an unbalanced picture of Jesus. They have selected only the prettier scenes of the Gospel. They picture Jesus only as the one who forgives sinners, heals the blind, the deaf and the sick and blesses children. But they overlook those parts of the Gospel—especially as found in Mark and John—which portray him confronting people. In order to carry out his mission of revealing the kingdom, Jesus had to confront the scribes and Pharisees when they misled the people. Jesus knew the risk he was taking, a risk that led ultimately to his death. In speaking the truth, he confronted the religious leaders and political power of his culture, but those who were open to his truth heard and accepted his message.

Our cultural values and attitudes portrayed through the media are an obstacle to accepting the *real* Jesus who confronts untruth wherever he finds it. The media present the ideal human person as cool, unruffled, and always pleasant. It pictures the *good* person as one who never causes pain for some greater good. To accept this idol as our ideal without criticizing it can lead to the illusory policy of "peace at any price." Madonna lived by this policy and thus became its victim.

For the excessively retiring person, there are certain aids to approach a more balanced behavior. Many schools have courses in self-assertiveness, in confrontational skills, and in conflict resolution. All these techniques, helpful as they may be, presuppose much ego-strength in the person. To use these skills well, one has to possess a sense of one's inner worth and mission. Furthermore, one has to be sensitive to, and reverent toward, the other person. For if just relations are to be achieved and maintained, some conflictual encounters are indispensable. Given human limitations, the inability to grasp the whole truth, misunderstandings, and weakness of will, it should not be surprising that situations arise demanding some assertiveness. Facing up to another with respect, firmness, gentleness and perhaps a little humor provides the opportunity for growth in justice.

To become truly human and Christian always requires courage. It is very challenging to keep seeking that delicate balance between the extreme of over-passivity (withdrawing from conflicts) and the opposite extreme of aggressiveness, often involving violence of heart and action. It is usually assumed that the scenes of excessive violence portrayed in the media cause viewers to become more violent in their relationships with others. This may be one response to violence but certain personalities react by resolving *never* to be violent. Unfortunately this resolve may be translated into a policy of never being forceful. Then caught in the fear of being hurt even more than of hurting others, one sets no limit to patience, moving to the area where patience ceases to be a virtue.

To yield to any hatred, contempt or neglect of persons is to swing to the opposite extreme. This attitude expresses itself in uncontrolled violent emotions, words, and physical force disrespectful of the other's person. This attitude expressed itself in the late 1960's in the fad of being frank at all costs. Sometimes the truth was expressed both frankly and destructively. For instance, in one college class, a freshman blurted out to his novice instructor what a "bummer" of a teacher he was. The freshman was being frank, indeed, without giving any thought to the consequences. He failed to consider that this manner of sharing his verdict might easily drive the teacher, not to patient steady improvement, but to withdraw from the classroom forever—which, in fact, was what actually took place.

The aggressive person mistakenly believes that one should insist single-mindedly on one's own rights. Such an individual overlooks the duty to respect others' rights and those of the common good. Such a person implicitly assumes that every claim to a right is a *just* claim. The urge to total independence and unbounded self-reliance has led many Americans of the more dominant type to this second extreme. In turn, this power position has pushed weaker, more passive Americans toward the first extreme. It is an ongoing task to keep striving for the balance of a mature, socially conscious claiming of one's rights and the fulfilling of one's responsibilities.

Questions for Your Reflection

1. On a scale ranging from the overly passive to the overly aggressive where would you place yourself?
2. What positive actions can you take to move toward

that delicate balance point between passivity and aggression?

3. What experiences have you had confronting others? What was the result of your confrontation?

4. Recall some situations when you have been confronted. How did you react in these situations?

A TWENTIETH CENTURY WITNESS

As a child, Eleanor Roosevelt was nicknamed "Granny" by her mother because she was such a shy, serious child. When Eleanor was eight, her mother died and she was sent to live with her maternal grandmother. Her grandmother was very strict, so Eleanor grew up fearing authority even more than she feared water, dark, and high mountains. She was so frightened of people that at the age of eighteen, shortly after the beginning of her own debutante party, she ran to her room to avoid her guests.

About this time, Eleanor decided she was too ugly to attract young men and that her only hope for friends was to associate with others interested in causes. She joined a group of Junior League girls and started teaching dancing to children in the New York slums. She was terrified as she walked through the Bowery and saw strange people living in conditions she never imagined existed. Instead of withdrawing, she worked to overcome her fears and gradually became more independent and emotionally mature.

In spite of her involvement in countless social justice causes Eleanor was never completely free of her shyness and fears. When her husband, Franklin D. Roosevelt, was elected president of the United States in 1932, she found it difficult to share in his victory celebrations, since she felt so inadequate and unprepared to be "First Lady." But even during her first year in the White House, the columnist Westbrook Pegler commented that White House protocol had become less important because "Mrs. Roosevelt has been too busy with such undignified trivialities as old-age pension, a ban on child labor and the protection of health of mothers and children."

In her autobiography, Eleanor explained how she had come to her world vision in these words: "One curious thing is that I have always seen life personally; that is, my interest or sympathy or indignation is not aroused by an abstract cause but by the plight of a single person whom I have seen with my own eyes. It was the sight of a child dying of hunger that made the tragedy of hunger become of such overriding importance to me. Out of my response to an individual develops an awareness of a problem to the community, and finally to the world. In each case my feeling of obligation to do something has stemmed from one individual and then widened and become applied to a broader area" (*Autobiography*, p. 413).

Questions for Your Reflection

1. How do you explain that someone as shy and fearful as Eleanor could become known throughout the world for her courageous involvement in social justice?
2. How do you react to Eleanor's process of moving to a world vision—starting with an individual, then the community and finally including the world?
3. Have you had any experiences where the injustice suffered by one person has opened new horizons for you? Did these new horizons include the community and the world? Explain in what way.

CALL TO ACTION

1. As you read the newspaper or listen to newscasts this coming week make a list of situations that strike you as unjust.

2. Try to get in touch with your feelings about each of these situations. Record your feelings next to each event in your list.

3. What could be done to insure greater justice in each of the situations you have noticed?

3. *Saul of Tarsus*

SCENE ONE

Saul, a short, twenty-eight year old, sharp-featured Jew, clasps in his fist a parchment scroll giving him the authority to search out and arrest members of the new Jewish sect. There, inside Jerusalem's Damascus Gate, he is instructing his team of fellow pursuers for their trek up north. His flashing black hair and piercing eyes radiate how eager he is to maintain and defend the strict observance of his Jewish religion by all Jews.

Reared in Tarsus (in present-day Turkey), Saul is a Roman citizen because of his father. But born of a Jewish mother, he had come to Jerusalem to be schooled in Judaism. Among the Pharisees, a group known for its strict observance of the Mosaic law, Saul stood out for his intelligence and fidelity to his Jewish heritage.

Toward the close of his studies, however, Saul encountered a growing disorder in Judaism. The trouble stemmed from a dissident sect, Galilean in origin, made up of the followers of a certain Jesus from Nazareth. The chief priests and Pharisees had rid themselves of Jesus, and Saul himself had personally witnessed and approved the stoning of that troublesome preacher of this sect, Stephen by name. Yet the group kept growing like some poisonous weed in Jerusalem, Judea, and now even in

Damascus. Saul, as a fervent, even fanatical, Pharisee, fully dedicated to the law of Moses, had committed himself to eradicate the followers of that sect. He was convinced that the only way to keep Judaism pure was to ferret out these Jesus-followers and to lock them up in prisons.

Ready for his mission to Damascus, Saul does not recognize how he has been trapped by the prescriptions of the Mosaic law. His schooling has drilled the law and its details into his mind, catching him in its system. Without realizing it his spirit has become more imprisoned than the Christian women, men and children his zeal has put behind bars. He is so busy carrying out orders from above that he hasn't taken time to examine and criticize how this system fits in with Moses' Lord who frees the oppressed. He has accepted a power structure's commission to wipe out the disciples of Jesus. Now, directed by that power, Saul believes that he is the one chosen to straighten things out. Furthermore, his accomplishments are winning him more prestige and influence. He has even been accepted into the inner circle of the Pharisees and high priests. The sealed parchment in his hand is proof enough of that.

INTERLUDE

In a blaze of light, the Lord Jesus reveals himself to Saul on his journey to Damascus. Humbled, Saul enters the city, is greeted as "Brother Saul" by Ananias, and is baptized into the community of the Christians. Soon Saul surprises Christians and traditional Jews alike by boldly proclaiming that "Jesus is indeed Lord."

SCENE TWO

Four years later, Saul, now called Paul, is preaching to a mixed group of Christians in a home in Damascus. He is more aware than they that he is the former persecutor of Christ's own body, the Church. Yet he also knows that he is a person loved and chosen by Jesus Christ. For the risen Lord has selected Paul and entrusted him to be his apostle to the Gentiles. Paul tells his audience that he is both an ambassador of Christ and a vivid example of God's merciful forgiveness. Paul's face radiates his gratitude and joy at having been transformed by the Spirit into a Christian and an apostle to the Gentiles. He has already experienced that being faithful to his mission means he must undergo much suffering, controversy, mistrust and attempts on his life.

Now, Paul's great talents and fiery personality have a different tone about them. He is tender toward widows and orphans. He is adventurous yet patient. The Spirit urges him to bring the good news of Christ's love to still more remote regions. When confronting or outmaneuvering the Pharisees and other Jews who plot against his life, he is bold and daring. He now describes his life as "being seized by the Lord Jesus and, in turn, trying to seize Jesus." And in this vital process, Paul's personality reflects the Lord Jesus more and more each day.

Questions for Your Reflection

1. In Scene One, what qualities did Saul exhibit that would later make him a good apostle?

2. The word "conversion" means a turning around. If Saul's personality remained basically the same, how was he "turned around"?

3. According to Vatican II, the Church must undergo continuous conversion. What responsibility does this place on every Christian adult? How do you experience this responsibility in your life?

4. Since Christians are called each year during Lent to fuller conversion to Christ, along what lines should one expect that conversion to occur?

5. In what ways does a Christian recognize the call to ongoing conversion?

An Experiment

Jot down briefly your answers to the following questions so that later you can reflect on them more easily. In each instance, knowing yourself, *predict* as realistically as you can (a) what inside feelings and urges you would experience and (b) what your behavior would be.

1. Approaching a movie theater, you discover a long line of people waiting for tickets. Near the head of the line, a friend of yours unexpectedly waves to you and, backing up a bit, makes room for you to enter.

2. You happen on a copy of *Playboy* on a coffee table.

3. You're in a conversation with a person whose talk is leading toward backbiting a mutual friend.

4. To the trio scoring highest in the Graduate Record Exam in your city, three full four-year scholarships will be awarded. As you take your place to write this exacting four-hour exam, you find that the most intelligent girl in your school is sitting directly in front or you. Moreover, she is so small and you are so tall that, even without making a move, you can easily see how she's marking her test.

5. After the Saturday night party, you climb into Bill's car with two other friends. You soon find Bill driving 70 mph in zones marked 40 mph and he has already run two red lights. You also know that Bill is hot-headed and doesn't take correction easily.

Questions on the Above Experiment

1. For each of the situations compare part a of your response to part b. What does this comparison tell you about yourself?
2. Are spontaneous feelings, not yet under your control, either morally good or morally bad? If not, when do these feelings take on a moral quality?
3. How can spontaneous feelings be a call to conversion? What helps are available to us to respond as a genuine Christian?

GOSPEL EVENT

"Jesus left Judea and went back to Galilee. This meant that he had to cross Samaria. On the way he came to the Samaritan town called Sychar, near the land that Jacob gave to his son Joseph. Joseph's well is there and Jesus, tired by the journey, sat straight down by the well. It was about the sixth hour (noon). When a Samaritan woman came to draw water, Jesus said to her, 'Give me a drink.' His disciples had gone into the town to buy food. The Samaritan woman said to him, 'What? You are a Jew and you ask me, a Samaritan, for a drink?' Jews, in fact, do not associate with Samaritans. Jesus replied: 'If you only knew what God is offering and who it is that is saying to you: "Give me a drink," you would have been the one to ask, and he would have given you living water.'

" 'You have no bucket, sir,' she answered, 'and the well is deep: how could you get this living water? Are you a greater man than our father Jacob who gave us this well and drank from it himself with his sons and his cattle?'

"Jesus replied, 'Whoever drinks this water will get thirsty again; but anyone who drinks the water that I shall give will never be thirsty again: the water that I shall give will turn into a spring inside him welling up to eternal life.'

" 'Sir,' said the woman 'give me some of that water, so that I may never have to come here again to draw water.'

" 'Go and call your husband,' said Jesus to her, 'and come back here.' The woman answered, 'I have no husband.' He said to her, 'You are right to say, "I have no husband," for although you have had five, the one you have now is not your husband. You spoke the truth there.'

" 'I see you are a prophet, sir,' said the woman. 'Our fathers worshiped on this mountain, while you say that Jerusalem is the place where one ought to worship.'

"Jesus said: 'Believe me, woman, the hour is coming when you will worship the Father neither on this mountain nor in Jerusalem. You worship what you do not know; we worship what we do know; for salvation comes from the Jews. But the hour will come—in fact it is here already—when true worshipers will worship the Father in spirit and truth; that is the kind of worshiper the Father wants. God is spirit, and those who worship must worship in spirit and truth.'

"The woman said to him, 'I know that the Messiah— that is, Christ—is coming, and when he comes he will tell us everything.'

" 'I who am speaking to you,' said Jesus, 'I am he.'

"At this point his disciples returned, and were surprised to find him speaking to a woman, though none of them asked, 'What do you want from her?' or 'Why are you talking to her?' The woman put down her water jar and hurried back to the town to tell the people, 'Come and see a man who has told me everything I ever did; I wonder if he is the Christ.' This brought people out of the town and they started walking toward him . . . .

"Many Samaritans of that town had believed in him on the strength of the woman's testimony when she said, 'He told me all I have ever done,' so, when the Samaritans came up to him, they begged him to stay with them. He stayed for two days, and when he spoke to them, many more came to believe; and they said to the woman, 'Now we no longer believe because of what you told us; we have heard him ourselves and we know that he really is the Savior of the world' " (John 4:1–30, 39–42).

Questions for Your Reflection

1. As the scene opens, how would you describe the quality of life of the Samaritan woman?
2. How did Jesus' way of speaking with the woman promote the change occurring in her?
3. Trace the steps of the Samaritan woman's conversion.
4. Describe how the Samaritan woman's growth depends on her being more respectful and honest to herself and to the stranger at the well.
5. In what ways was the Samaritan woman's conversion similar to Paul's? In what ways do these two examples of conversion differ?
6. What indications do you find that the Samaritan woman is growing: (a) as a truth-seeker? (b) as a woman who uses her affective responses better? (c) as a morally transformed person? (d) as a religiously deepened woman?
7. Recall times when you experienced the call to grow in any of the ways mentioned in #6. How did you recognize the call?

A WORD OF CHRISTIAN WITNESS

William Shakespeare was one who saw deeply into the human person. He had one of his characters advise: "To thine own self be true and it follows as night the day that thou canst be false to no man." Being true to oneself is recognizing and using one's sound potentials and gifts. It also involves realizing that in spite of wayward tendencies our loving Father creates, affirms and protects each person.

The forces of darkness both within and beyond the human person cast shadows over the deepest, most authentic self. Then, too, one tends to shy away from seeing the fuller truth about oneself. One fears that such a sight will hurt—forgetting that the hurt is just the first step toward healing. Avoiding the truth of oneself, trying to escape the difficulties of life, leads to self-centering. One may become locked in a personal world and grow cold to most others. Slogans, expressed and implicit, promoting this self-centering bombard the individual from every side. The media is constantly saying in many ways: "Look out for number 1," "Get them before they get you," "Push ahead before others step on you." It's little wonder, then, that there are self-serving individualists in our world today.

William James described such an individualist as a "sick-souled self." The person feels divided inside, out of touch with his or her better self. Even while looking out for one's own good, there may be a sense that others are not being treated fairly, that one is not really fair to oneself either. Inner motivation is lacking to get in touch with that self, or to seek the truth steadfastly. The wish to love others more faithfully and reverently may be present but it's too hard. One may want to respond to the Holy Spirit, but there is the suspicion that he's not for real. Feeling the weight of increasing weakness of will, the unfree soul may groan or perhaps whimper or sigh for escape but make no real effort to move to freedom.

How is escape from such self-illusion possible? If there is a readiness to respond to the Holy Spirit, sometimes an escape simply breaks through. Perhaps one finds greater freedom through a period of great suffering which allows the Spirit's enlightenment to shine through. This breakthrough often has qualities that are reminiscent of Paul's conversion. It is sudden, surprising and powerful, leaving no doubt that a response is called for.

More commonly, perhaps, the breakthrough is gradual, at times almost imperceptible, but nonetheless real. The insistent but kind question of some genuine friend may bring the awareness of a glimmer of light at the end of a tunnel leading out of darkness. Or reflection upon an experience in which one narrowly escaped serious danger, such as a nearly fatal auto accident, may show how one has been trapped in illusion.

With the recognition of being trapped in illusion comes the awareness that one can't get out of this mess alone. The Holy Spirit is needed to clear away the fog that keeps one from the full truth, to empower one to make necessary changes. Here is the moment of conversion. However and whenever the call comes, the task is to pray and to respond as fully as possible. Daily, and even hourly, responses to the Spirit's invitations make up one's ongoing conversion and make a person grow in building justice in self.

Questions for Your Reflection

1. Why is it important to be just to oneself?
2. Can a person who is not just to oneself be just to others?
3. How might an individualist move toward becoming a just person?
4. What part does truth play in the conversion process?

A TWENTIETH CENTURY WITNESS

Harry is twenty-two years old now, has average intelligence and, after investing nearly a year elsewhere, is once again working toward his college degree. It happened this way. Harry's family is strict and traditional. Harry's final years in high school and first year in college were a time of crisis for him. He felt his parents' restrictions more and more each month and he no longer believed in their values. He also grew increasingly angry even at such little things as his brother's and sister's teasing.

Harry had heard of a group of young people who lived together fifteen miles outside town. One day he simply packed up, left home without notice and went to join the group. During his first weeks there he fell in love with this new life-style. What a glorious escape from family and college routine! All the members of this group lived and let live, played it cool and went with the flow. There was no privacy and everything seemed to belong to everyone. Food? Pass it around. Drink? Pass it around. Pot? Pass it around. Girls? Pass 'em around. At first he felt some qualms about living this way but his companions had more experience than he in these matters and so knew better. As the months passed, Harry became more like his companions every day. He became disheveled; his jeans became ragged. After six months he had become as hooked on drugs and sexual indulgence as they were. And with each day his sense of escaping into freedom grew dimmer, like a fading honeymoon.

Then one morning, he somehow got up before the others. He tried to wash the sleep and hangover from his eyes. What he saw in the mirror made him stop and look more closely. Then it happened. Was the person he saw before him really himself? What had happened to those eyes? to that face? Inside, Harry felt that somehow he both knew and didn't know that face in the mirror. What a strange revulsion he felt inside! Shocked at what he saw, he asked himself, "Is this really the person I want to be? What's happening to my talents?" Like lightning the truth bore into him. He was wasting his life. Horrified at seeing how much he had squandered of himself and his gifts during the last months, he knew he had to change. Moving into action, he quietly stepped over the sleeping bodies strewn on the floor, hitched a ride back to town, and left a message with his family about where they could find him. He "bit the bullet" by handing himself over to a detoxification center. Soon he was working at a summer job making money for re-entry into college. Now he wants to give his inner gifts a real chance to grow in responsible freedom. Now he is convinced that this is the way to develop more life in greater freedom.

Questions for Your Reflection

1. Do you know any case like Harry's? How did the turnaround occur?
2. Inside Harry, what happened as he looked into the mirror?
3. What kind of getting in touch with his deeper self did it take for Harry to start believing more in his own inner life-potentials than in what his friends told him?
4. Was the Holy Spirit at work during Harry's experience in front of the mirror? Before it? After it? What signs make you say "yes" or "no"?
5. Psychologists say that a person can be fair to oneself only if one is so deeply in touch with oneself that one lets his or her own reality shed the light of its truth into one's consciousness. Can you identify the instances where Harry seemed untrue to his better self? and the instances

39

where he became deeply enough in touch with his better self?

6. When you experience within yourself some interests and calls that pull you to be untrue to your more authentic self, and others pulling you in the opposite direction, how do you deal with these movements that tug at your heart?

CALL TO ACTION

1. Look into a mirror penetratingly yet lovingly and ask whether you see potentials untapped or wasted in yourself. What do you find?

2. What can you do to counter self-illusion and become your truer self?

3. Ask your best friend or close counselor to point out the attitude or tendency in you which, if left unwatched, might bring you harm sooner or later. Can you find some past experiences in your life illustrating that attitude and tendency? How can you work against it?

4. John

John, a junior in college, is running for student council president. He is a hard-working, efficient student and is putting a lot of time and energy into his campaign. It is very important to his self-image that he succeed in winning this office. He knows that future employers will be impressed to see "student council president" on his resume among his academic and athletic achievements.

John owes his success-oriented attitude toward life to his parents. From earliest childhood they impressed on him the importance of getting ahead in the world. "You might have to use a few people along the way, but do it with finesse," his father advised him. They praised him for his accomplishments, rewarded him for good grades in school and always encouraged him to do even better. They taught him good manners, and insisted that he be well-groomed. His parents impressed on him the importance of responding graciously to all kinds of people so that they would like him. They had trained John well, were proud of their son and would be even happier with him if he became student council president.

John knows that he has the support of the best students on campus—those who are intelligent and hard-working, those who want the most out of life. He has a feeling that there are other members of the student body who are jealous of his good looks, his academic rank and his athletic awards. In fact, he suspects that they think he is a conceited show-off. If he is going to win the election he will have to appeal to these students too. In order to win their votes he will have to hide his contempt for them, and not indicate in any way that he thinks they are lazy and stupid. For a while, until after the elections, he will have to pretend to be their friend. He knows how to tell them the things they want to hear. He has ways of making them believe that he is one of them. He knows it will be hard but he can do it; he has done hard things before to succeed.

Questions for Your Reflection

1. Have you ever met anyone like John? How do you react to such a person?

2. If John continues this pattern, how do you think his character will be affected?

3. What does John need to do to change his pattern of behavior?

4. What Christian principles are being violated in the way John is carrying on his campaign?

An Experiment

1. Take the time to go to a place where there are many kinds of people coming and going—perhaps a bus station, the public library or even a supermarket. Look at the people carefully, noting your inner feelings to various types of people. Jot down a one-line description of each person and number these descriptions from 1 to 10.

2. Next to the following statements put the number or numbers that apply from your list of ten descriptions.

  a. I am afraid of this person _____

  b. I would like to know this person _____

  c. I would welcome this person into my home _____

  d. I would help this person in case of need _____

e. I think this person might help me get ahead ____
f. I don't trust this person _____
3. On what have you based your responses in #2?
4. What does this experiment tell you about yourself?

GOSPEL EVENT

In order to appreciate this event in the life of Jesus it is necessary to understand the historical setting. At this time the Jews were subject to Rome, a governor having been appointed to rule over them and to keep peace. The governor lived with the constant fear of an uprising that would reflect on his ability to govern. He allowed the Jews some semblance of freedom and did not interfere with their customs and religious practices as long as they did not cause any disturbance.

One of the ways the Romans had of avoiding trouble, and at the same time humiliating the Jews, was forcing the Jews to collect taxes from their own people. The tax collectors were looked upon as collaborators with Rome and therefore were detested by their own people. They also made their living by increasing the taxes so that their take was substantial after the Roman quotas were met. Many tax collectors became wealthy men but they were scorned as oppressors and traitors. Zacchaeus not only was a tax collector but it is thought that he had bought the privilege of being the superintendent of tax collectors.

"He (Jesus) entered Jericho and was going through the town when a man whose name was Zacchaeus made his appearance; he was one of the senior tax collectors and a wealthy man. He was anxious to see what kind of man Jesus was, but he was too short and could not see him for the crowd; so he ran ahead and climbed a sycamore tree to catch a glimpse of Jesus who was to pass that way.

When Jesus reached the spot he looked up and spoke to him: 'Zacchaeus, come down. Hurry, because I must stay at your house today.' And he hurried down and welcomed him joyfully. They all complained when they saw what was happening. 'He has gone to stay at a sinner's house,' they said. But Zacchaeus stood his ground and said to the Lord, 'Look, sir, I am going to give half my property to the poor, and if I have cheated anybody I will pay him back four times the amount.' And Jesus said to him, 'Today salvation has come to this house, because this man too is a son of Abraham; for the Son of Man has come to seek out and save what was lost' " (Luke 19:1–10).

As the people crowded along the roadside to see Jesus, Zacchaeus was pushed into the background. He was despised and ignored by the very people who were acclaiming Jesus. Since he was short he was unable to see from the back row where he had been pushed. Nevertheless he desired so much to see Jesus that he used his ingenuity to find a way.

Questions for Your Reflection

    1. Suppose you were standing along the road waiting to see Jesus. How would you feel about Zacchaeus?
    2. Imagine yourself in the place of Zacchaeus. What would be your attitude toward the crowd? toward Jesus?
    3. How did Jesus respond to Zacchaeus?
    4. Are there any similarities between this event and an experience in your life?
    5. After his encounter with Jesus, Zacchaeus changed his way of relating to the poor and to taxpayers. How can you change your inter-personal relations to make them more just?

The two incidents presented here for your reflection involve an attitude that is basic to justice. It is the foundation without which justice cannot exist or begin to grow. Without a recognition of the dignity of each human person any relationships with others will be lacking in justice. They will be manipulative, exploitative or oppressive. There is no way those relationships can be fair if the very foundation for fairness is missing.

The Pastoral Constitution on the Church in the Modern World expands on the truth of human worth and dignity. It is realistic in recognizing that the image of God in human beings has been tarnished by sin. But that is not the end of the story. Our dignity has been even more enhanced. Through the passion and death of Jesus we are offered freedom and strength.

One might think that God's image is only in the intellect and will, a spiritual basis for human dignity. However, the Council fathers point out that the innate dignity of the individual extends to the body too. It is because we have material bodies that we can gather together all of material creation and offer it back to God. As Paul wrote to the Romans, "The whole creation is eagerly waiting for God to reveal his sons. It was not for any fault on the part of creation that it was made unable to attain its purpose, it was made so by God; but creation still retains the hope of being freed, like us, from its slavery to decadence, to enjoy the same freedom and glory as the children of God" (Romans 8:19–22).

The Council fathers did not hesitate to state that "authentic freedom is an exceptional sign of the divine image" within the human person. In freedom the human intellect reflects the image of God as it searches for the truth. By reflection on these insights of the Council fathers a person comes to a deeper realization of the magnificent value of each individual. In the light of these truths let us take another look at John, Jesus and Zacchaeus.

John is the kind of person who is motivated by the importance of his own self-image. His relationships are not based on a recognition that he and all others have been created in the image of God and therefore have dignity. Because of this innate dignity all people are worthy of respect and deserve to be treated accordingly.

John has so identified with his image of himself as the successful one, the organizer, the achiever that he operates out of this false image rather than his true self. He is deceiving himself, as well as the others he manipulates, to support his false identity. In the incident presented here John has assumed the role of student leader. He is the type of person who will easily adopt other roles that he perceives as enhancing his image of success. He is always on the alert for whatever "works." People of this type seldom express their true feelings. They express feelings appropriate to the occasion; they behave as other people expect them to act so that they will be liked. Their greatest fear is failure, especially failure in relationships.

John would have a difficult time relating to Zacchaeus, for Zacchaeus was not concerned about his self-image. He knew that he was unpopular with the crowd; he realized that he would look comical clinging to the branches of the sycamore tree in order to see Jesus. He was true to himself; he really desired to *see* Jesus—nothing more. He had no ulterior motive; he was not thinking of ways Jesus could be of service to him or enhance his reputation. He just wanted "to see Jesus" and he used the available means with a total lack of human respect.

Jesus looked up in the sycamore tree and invited himself to dinner at Zacchaeus' home. Jesus saw the innate dignity of this so-called "sinner." The people in the crowd were scandalized that Jesus would eat with a tax collector. Like John they looked down on people who did not meet their standards and refused respect to anyone who did not meet with their approval. Because Jesus saw a human person made to the image of his Father and treated Zacchaeus with respect, Zacchaeus responded by reaching deep within himself to that inner core of truth. He promised to change his life and to make restitution for the harm he had done to others. As a result of this encounter with Jesus he saw people differently. They were no longer the objects of his exploitation but individuals to be treated with fairness and respect. He saw the inner dignity of the poor, too, and realized that they deserved to live better than they were, so he shared half of all his wealth with them.

It is interesting to note that Jesus did not condemn the Roman tax system that provided so many opportunities for corruption. Neither did he demand that Zacchaeus give up his position of chief tax collector. However, he did expect Zacchaeus to act justly toward taxpayers and share his wealth with the poor.

In contrast to this universal love based on the image of God in each one, the Council fathers itemize some of the injustices that result from a lack of basic respect: "Furthermore, whatever is opposed to life itself, such as any type of murder, genocide, abortion, euthanasia, or willful self-destruction, whatever violates the integrity of the human person, such as mutilation, torments inflicted on body or mind, attempts to coerce the will itself, whatever insults human dignity, such as subhuman living conditions, arbitrary imprisonment, deportation, slavery, prostitution, the selling of women and children, as well as disgraceful working conditions, where men are treated as mere tools for profit, rather than as free and responsible persons—all these things and others of their like are infamies indeed. They poison human society, but they do more harm to those who practice them than those who suffer from the injury. Moreover, they are a supreme dishonor to the Creator" (*Pastoral Constitution on the Church in the Modern World,* II, # 27).

Questions for Your Reflection

1. Do you agree with the Council fathers that those who practice the injustices they enumerate do more harm to themselves than to those they injure? Give reasons for your answer.
2. Do you believe that a person can be just without being respectful of every human person? Give examples to substantiate your belief.
3. Do you see any structures in our society that resemble the Roman tax system in making corruption easy? Can a Christian live within these structures and respond justly? How?

A TWENTIETH CENTURY WITNESS

In December 1932, Dorothy Day was in Washington, D.C. to cover the communist demonstration. A friend had told her of the planned march to Washington. She was always alert for journalistic opportunities and proposed to *Commonweal* magazine that she cover the march and write the story for them. She had mixed feelings about the march—wishing she could join them, being sympathetic to their desire to help the poor, but recognizing that since she had become a Catholic she held some fundamental philosophical beliefs very different from her former communist beliefs.

After the demonstration she wrote her story and then went to the Shrine of the Immaculate Conception to pray, asking God to show her how she could use her talents to help the poor. As she prayed, she did not know how quickly and completely God would answer her prayer.

The next day she took the bus back to New York, looking forward to seeing her daughter Tamara. She arrived to find several friends and a stranger awaiting her. Later, she was to write her first impressions of this stranger, Peter Maurin. She wrote that he was "a short, broad-shouldered workingman with a high, broad head covered with greying hair. His face was weather-beaten, he had warm grey eyes and a wide, pleasant mouth. The collar of his shirt was dirty, but he had tried to dress up by wearing a tie and a suit which looked as though he had slept in it."

In spite of his appearance, Dorothy invited Peter to supper, and he then explained how he had been looking for Dorothy for some time. He knew of her background of socialism and communism and her recent conversion to the Catholic Church. He believed that she needed a Catholic education and he was there to give it to her. He also had in mind that Dorothy would be just the one to begin a Catholic labor paper.

Dorothy and Peter were to collaborate for many years in the Catholic Worker movement, publishing the penny paper and establishing houses of hospitality in numerous cities in the United States and even in Europe. Dorothy's acceptance of Peter was symbolic of the thousands who came seeking shelter and finding a warm welcome.

The remainder of Dorothy's life reflected the way God answered her prayer at the Shrine of the Immaculate Conception in December 1932. She saw in each person she met the image of Christ, a person to be respected and loved. She found it very difficult to understand those who were forever studying the problem of poverty without loving and respecting the poor.

The Catholic Worker movement was built on the realization that each individual has been created by God and redeemed by Christ. This basic truth was the orientation for their approach to social problems. They believed in the primacy of Christian love to affect the process of history and to change it for the better. Dorothy often quoted the words of Dostoevsky in *The Brothers Karamazov:* "Love in action is a harsh and dreadful thing compared to love in dreams . . . . Active love is labor and fortitude, and for some people, too, perhaps a complete science. But I predict that just when you see with horror that in spite of all your efforts you are getting further from your goal instead of nearer to it—at that very moment you will reach and behold clearly the miraculous power of the Lord who has been all the time loving and mysteriously guiding you."

Questions for Your Reflection

1. If you returned from a trip to find a neighbor whom you find unattractive waiting for you in your home, how would you respond?

2. Later Dorothy described Peter as "a genius, a saint, an agitator, a writer, a lecturer, a poor man, and a shabby tramp, all in one." Suppose you met someone that fit this description. Would you see the "genius, the saint, the writer, the lecturer," or would you see just a "shabby tramp"?

3. What do you look for when you choose your friends or the people you wish to associate with socially or in various kinds of activities?

4. Compare Dorothy's view of love with popular conceptions of love. Do they have anything in common?

CALL TO ACTION

Sometime during the coming week have a conversation with a person with whom you would not ordinarily associate. Exchange some ideas with this person and notice your feelings at the beginning and at the end of your conversation. What have you learned from this encounter?

5. Tom

Tom is a young executive in a corporation. He is very intelligent and ambitious and has worked himself into an important position in the personnel office. He prides himself on living by the rules, and his employers feel that they can depend on him to follow corporate policy. He is loyal to the company and to his boss.

The corporation is an equal opportunity employer, and Tom sincerely believes that women should be treated as equals on the job. He has even urged management to pay women equal wages for equal work. He has initiated a merit system in the corporation to insure that women have an equal opportunity for advancement. Through his efforts women are treated with greater respect by their fellow male workers, for they know that if the women have any complaints they will be given a fair hearing. When asked why he has helped women in his corporation, Tom always answers, "It's the law, you know."

Tom has been married to Debbie for ten years. Their two children are in school now and Debbie would like to go back to work. She is a teacher and she has pointed out to Tom that her work time would coincide with the childrens' school day so she would not be neglecting the children by working. Tom absolutely refuses to even consider it. He tells her that a woman's place is in the home; he makes enough to support the family. He reminds her that St. Paul said, "The man is the head of the family."

Tom does not understand that it is important for Debbie to go back to teaching. He gives her everything she needs, and is usually a considerate, loving husband and father as long as his authority is not threatened. He likes security. He worries a lot but feels that the family is his responsibility, so he does not share his worries with his wife. He is the one who must make the decisions, and he is very careful to check out all the possibilities so he can be sure he is doing the right thing.

Tom loves his children very much. Tom, Jr. is allowed to do almost everything he wants to do. Tom believes that his son needs to be independent, to learn to make his own decisions. He needs to be able to take care of himself. Tom becomes upset with Debbie because he thinks Debbie sometimes babies their son. She tries to comfort him if he's been hurt but Tom shouts at him, "Don't you dare cry! Be a man!"

Tom is very different with his daughter Jane. He protects her and doesn't want her to grow up or to decide anything for herself. Tom, Jr. resents the way his father treats Jane. He tells his friends, "She's spoiled rotten!" Debbie believes that Jane should learn to take responsibility as well as Tom, Jr. Tom and Debbie have many arguments about the best way to raise their children.

Questions for Your Reflection

1. Is there consistency in the way Tom is acting? If so, what is the basis of that consistency?
2. If you were in Tom's place would you feel hurt and angry if someone accused you of being unjust to your wife?
3. Is Tom being fair to his children? Is he wise in wanting Tom, Jr., but not Jane, to be independent?
4. What could Tom do to make his relationship with the members of his family more just?

An Experiment*

Picture the following five scenes in your mind's eye:

(1) A business executive dictates a letter to a secretary.
(2) A surgeon asks a nurse for a scalpel.
(3) A homemaker directs a plumber to a troublesome toilet.
(4) A professor has an affair with a student.
(5) A high school principal counsels an art teacher.

Suppose now that you are a personnel officer responsible for your firm's hiring for various positions. Reflect on the way you pictured the five scenes above. Ask yourself the sex your picture gave to the persons in each pair. For example, in #1, was the executive a man or a woman? Was the secretary a man or a woman? Continue in the same way with the remaining four scenes.

If you discover that you automatically put men into certain professions and women into others, are you unconsciously discriminating as a personnel officer? Is sexist prejudice deeper than our conscious efforts to be fair? How do people go about countering their unfair, indeliberate prejudices?

GOSPEL EVENT

"At daybreak Jesus appeared in the temple again; and as all the people came to him, he sat down and began to teach them.

"The scribes and Pharisees brought a woman along who had been caught committing adultery; and making

---

*Derived from an experiment designed by Professor Mary Mahowald of Case Western Reserve University.

54

her stand there in full view of everybody, they said to Jesus, 'Master, this woman was caught in the very act of committing adultery, and Moses has ordered us in the law to condemn women like this to death by stoning. What have you to say?' They asked him this as a test, looking for something to use against him. But Jesus bent down and started writing on the ground with his finger. As they persisted with their question, he looked up and said, 'If there is one of you who has not sinned, let him be the first to throw a stone at her.' Then he bent down and wrote on the ground again. When they heard this they went away one by one, beginning with the eldest, until Jesus was left alone with the woman, who remained standing there. He looked up and said, 'Woman, where are they? Has no one condemned you?' 'No one, sir,' she replied. 'Neither do I condemn you,' said Jesus. 'Go away, and don't sin any more'" (John 8:1–11).

Questions for Your Reflection

1. Are there any indications that the woman in this incident is being treated unjustly?
2. Do you believe that this woman should have been punished? If so, how should she be punished?
3. What does the fact that the man is not mentioned say to you about equal justice under the law?
4. How does the attitude of Jesus toward the law differ from Tom's concern for the law in the first situation?
5. Are there any situations today that resemble this incident in the life of Jesus? How are women treated in these situations?

A WORD OF CHRISTIAN WITNESS

If we compare the way the women in these two incidents of Tom and of Jesus with the adulteress are treated, we might be left with a feeling of hope. For it seems that the lot of women has improved since the time of Jesus. The self-righteous scribes and Pharisees were very ready to punish the woman they brought to Jesus. Apparently they were not concerned about the man involved nor were they conscious of their own sinfulness. Jesus, on the other hand, did not condone the woman's sin but he treated her with compassion and forgiveness. She was a person worthy of his mercy, for she had value in his eyes.

The scribes and the Pharisees were operating out of a level of justice based on the authority of the law. The law of Moses stated that such a person should be stoned, and they believed in abiding by the law. The justice of Jesus transcended all human levels of justice. Jesus did not fall into the trap his enemies had laid for him. Faced with the dilemma of disregarding the law and being looked upon as an unfaithful Jew, or keeping the law and being accused of cruelty, Jesus worked justice through compassion and mercy.

The first case gives another example of a person whose principles of justice are based on outside authority. Although Tom is intelligent he is still dependent on the expectations of others. The law and his boss tell him that he must be fair to the women in the corporation and recognize their rights. Tom conforms to these judgments and feels that he is doing the right thing.

However, his wife is in a different kind of relationship to him and a different authority controls his conduct. At home Tom conforms to values which he believes are values of his church. In spite of his love for his wife, he is oppressing her, treating her as inferior to himself, as someone whose life he controls. He does not recognize that his wife is a person with dignity and the right to make decisions about her own life. He sees no inconsistency in his treatment of women because it never occurs to him to reflect on the source of the values on which his behavior is based.

Many men become angry at the very mention of the injustices women suffer in our society. In one sense they are justified because the problem is much deeper—the issue is really the injustice of sexism. When any person, man or woman, is discriminated against because of sex, that person is being treated unfairly. When our society sets up expectations for either women or men based only on sex, there is injustice involved. Job opportunities can be discriminatory for both men and women. The controlling factor for employment should be the ability to do the work, not the sex of the worker. The salary should be the same whether a woman or a man is hired for the position.

Even though men too may suffer from discrimination in certain cases, by far the majority of situations involve women. Historically, women have been considered the possession of men. They have been given the same status as children under the law, and even today, in spite of many improvements, they are still second class citizens. There is still a long way to go to overcome the inequalities in the judicial system, in business, in politics, in family life, in social customs and in the Church.

Feminists of all persuasions have suggested remedies, ranging from changing sexist language to attacking the very way we relate to God. Some even go so far as to say that Jesus is an obstacle to women's liberation. It seems that many of these attitudes reveal more about the repressed anger of some women than they are helpful in bringing about a more just society. In some cases the oppression of women would merely be transferred to men. The basic question seems to be, "How can we think about ourselves and our world in such a way that no one suffers from oppression because of sex?"

Instead of trying to identify issues of sexism and

counter them one by one, possibly a simpler solution might be to look at all people as God does. As God looks at the world what does he see? He sees his creatures who have been created to his image and likeness, endowed with the ability to know him, to know themselves and the world around them. They have the capacity to love their Creator, to love themselves and to love one another. They all belong to one human family, God's family. Because these children of God can also stray from their Father, Jesus came to proclaim the reign of God, to bring liberation and reconciliation to all. Everyone has the opportunity to enter into the death and rising of Jesus, to become one with him and share his glory in the kingdom fulfilled. As Paul wrote to the Romans: "The Spirit gives witness with our spirit that we are children of God. But if we are children, we are heirs as well: heirs of God, heirs with Christ, if only we suffer with him so as to be glorified with him" (Romans 8:16–17). In its barest essentials, this is the unity that binds us all together.

Within this unity of humanity, sex is only one of the factors which give diversity, and thus richness, to the unified whole. Other factors, such as race, nationality, age, environmental background, and genetic inheritance, plus the many and various gifts of mind and body, combine with sex to give a unique character to each individual. These factors qualify the way each person relates to God, to others, to the world and to self, but they do not take away the basic equality before God.

Unfortunately, sin has been introduced into the ideal balance of unity and diversity. Because of sinfulness and brokenness, instead of rejoicing in the richness of diversity, there is a tendency to fear differences. Society focuses on these differences and, through stereotyping, sets up power structures that favor some while oppressing others. These power structures assure not only the dominance of male over female, but also white over black, young over elderly, healthy over ill, rich over poor. The sinfulness of humanity has shattered the unity and harmony of God's creation, sexism being just one of the indications of this lack of harmony.

Questions for Your Reflection

1. Reflect on the various relationships in your life. Which ones seem to be based on equality? Which ones have a basis in a power structure? How do you feel about these relationships?
2. Give some examples of sex discrimination you have encountered at work, in your social life, in the Church.
3. What evidences of sex discrimination do you notice in the media?
4. In what ways are children being trained to fit stereotypic roles? What changes do you suggest in the early training of children to promote greater fairness in relationships?
5. How can you help people see the unity of all human persons and at the same time appreciate the richness of diversity?

A TWENTIETH CENTURY WITNESS

In her book *Lifeforce,* Jean Houston recalls her friendship with a man who had a profound influence on her life. Years later, even small details of that wonderful time remain etched in her memory as she tells her story.

When I was about thirteen, I used to run down Park Avenue in New York City, late for school. I was a great big overgrown girl, and one day I ran right into a rather frail old gentleman in his seventies and knocked the wind out of him. He laughed as I helped him to his feet and asked me in French-accented speech, "Are you planning to run like that for the rest of your life?"

"Yes, sir," I replied. "It looks that way."

"Well, bon voyage!" he said.

"Bon voyage!" I answered and sped on my way.

About a week later I was walking down Park Avenue with my fox terrier, Champ, and again I met the old gentleman.

"Ah," he greeted me, "my friend the runner, and with a fox terrier. I knew one like that many years ago in France. Where are you going?"

"Well, sir," I replied, "I'm taking Champ to Central Park."

"I will go with you," he informed me. "I will take my constitutional."

And thereafter, for about a year, the old gentleman and I would meet and walk together in Central Park. His name, as far as I could make out, was Mr. Thayer or Mr. Tayer.

The walks were magical and full of delight. Mr. Tayer had absolutely no self-consciousness and would suddenly fall on his knees and exclaim to me, "Jeanne [he always used the French form of her name], look at the caterpillar! What does the caterpillar think? Does he know what he is going to become? Eh, Jeanne—feel yourself to be a caterpillar. What will you be when you become a butterfly? The next stage, Jeanne. The next stage! Metamorphosis! It is so exciting."

His long, gothic, comic-tragic face would nod with wonder.

"Eh, Jeanne, look at the clouds! God's calligraphy in the sky! All that transformation—moving, changing, dissolving, becoming. Eh, Jeanne—are you a cloud? Be a cloud."

Or there was the time that Mr. Tayer and I leaned into the strong wind that suddenly whipped through Central Park, and he told me, "Jeanne, sniff the wind. The same wind may have once been sniffed by Jesus Christ, by Alexander, by Jeanne d'Arc. Sniff the wind once sniffed by Jeanne d'Arc. Sniff the tides of history!"

It was wonderful. People of all ages followed us around, laughing—not at us, but with us. Occasionally, Mr. Tayer would give short comical addresses on the history of Central Park rocks. More often he would address the rocks directly. "Ah, my friend the mica schist layer, do you remember when . . .?" He seemed to know an awful lot about old bones and rocks.

He seemed to know a great deal about spirals, too. Once I brought him the shell of a snail, and he waxed ecstatic for the better part of an hour. Snail shells and galaxies and the meanderings of rivers were taken up into a great hymn to the spiraling of spirit and matter. When he had finished, his voice dropped, and he whispered almost in prayer, "Omega . . . . omega . . . . omega . . . ."

But mostly Mr. Tayer was so full of vital sap and juice that he seemed to flow with everything. Always he saw the inter-connections between things—the way that everything in the universe, from fox terriers to mica schist to the mind of God, was related to everything else and was very, very good.

I remember coming home once and telling my mother, "Mother, I met my old man again, and when I am with him, I leave my littleness behind." For Mr Tayer looked at you as if you were God-in-hiding, and the love with which you were regarded was unconditional. In his presence one felt empowered to be who one really was.

And then one day I didn't see him anymore. I would frequently go and stand outside of the Church of St. Ignatius Loyola on Eighty-fourth Street and Park Avenue where I often met him, but he never came again.

In 1961 someone lent me a copy of a book titled *The Phenomenon of Man*. The book, from which the jacket had been removed, was strangely familiar in its concepts. Occasional words and expressions loomed up as echoes from my past. When later in the book, I came across the concept of the "omega point," I was certain. I asked to see the jacket of the book, looked at the author's picture, and, of course, recognized him immediately. There was no forgetting or mistaking that face. Mr. Tayer was Teilhard de Chardin, the great priest-scientist, poet, and mystic, and during that lovely and luminous year I had been meeting him outside the Jesuit rectory of St. Ignatius, where he was living at the time (Jean Houston, *Lifeforce*. New York: Delacorte Press, 1980, pp. 218–220).

In contrast to Tom, we see Teilhard, with his vast knowledge and experience, relating to a young girl as a person deserving his respect. His attitude had a powerful effect on Jean; she felt worthwhile and grown-up. Because she was not put down by this elderly, scholarly, kind gentleman, she experienced her dignity and value as a person.

Teilhard de Chardin has left us a hopeful vision of the world in his description of the spiraling movement of humanity in ever greater unity toward the Omega Point, Christ. The energizing force that is drawing us all closer together is love which must be the motivation underlying all our attitudes of justice toward one another. Teilhard could see glimmers of the actualization of Paul's faith statement to the Galatians: "All of you who have been baptized into Christ have clothed yourselves with him. There does not exist among you Jew or Greek, slave or freeman, male or female. All are one in Christ Jesus" (Galatians 3:27–28). Any indications that humanity was moving toward greater unity filled Teilhard with hope.

Questions for Your Reflection

1. What does this incident reveal about Teilhard's attitude toward women? toward teenagers?
2. What evidence do you find in the world that the energizing force of love is drawing people together?
3. How do you experience the energizing force of love in your life?
4. What steps can you take to lessen prejudice in yourself? in your family? in the place where you work?

CALL TO ACTION

1. Make a list of ten women you know. Next to each one jot down any evidences that these women are discriminated against because they are women.
2. What could you do to help one of these women counter the unjust discrimination she experiences?

6. *Melissa*

Melissa is a black woman, twenty-seven years old. She graduated cum laude from Wellesley, and after law school at the University of Michigan she passed the bar exam. She has dedicated herself to her people, especially to its younger members. Her chosen way of serving them is through the NAACP. Her well-prepared legal briefs won three recent local suits against discrimination for the NAACP.

Melissa often works eighteen hours a day, and sometimes there's no day off in her work-week. Her waking hours are jammed with the long hours at the NAACP office, with the care of her elderly grandfather and with many chores at home, along with the prolonged tutoring she does of high school blacks who want to enter quality colleges. Melissa's face has begun to show the pressure through the start of taut lines near her eyes. If she gets a few moments to relax, she enjoys gazing up at the citation of honor that hangs over her mantleplace. The Urban League gave it to her last year for distinguished service in reducing housing tensions in the city.

Sitting there one day, she hears a knock at her door. She opens it to find Charles Kraft, her landlord and white realtor. The memory flashes through her mind that this is the man who two years ago sold her relatives several 1890 houses at triple their price of purchase in 1970. This is also the man who served as a key witness against the

NAACP in one of last year's trials. Now he is telling Melissa that starting next week he is raising her rent twenty percent just as he is raising it for all the other lessees in his apartment buildings.

Melissa is usually a patient person. The high school students she tutors can vouch for that. If displeased or angry, she has learned through her work at Wellesley and Michigan to discipline herself against showing it. So she casually invites Mr. Kraft to explain some of the details necessitating the present rent hike and politely bids him goodbye.

However, once Kraft is gone, she paces back and forth planning how to use all her skills within legal limits to get even with this man. Soon she has phoned four friends to register official complaints against Mr. Kraft. The first will ask the fire department that it scrupulously inspect all Kraft's apartments since she sees exposed wiring, nonfunctional exit signs, and old fire hoses. Another friend will complain to the sanitation department that Kraft's garbage container facilities and periodic pest-control flagrantly violate current regulations and hence an inspection must be made. Melissa's close friend at the NAACP will instigate an investigation by the Equal Employment Opportunity Commission into Kraft's ten-year record of hiring women and minorities in his reality company and in his apartment building staffs. Melissa's fourth friend agrees to complain to the Internal Revenue Service that Mr. Kraft seems to be taking excessive depreciation on his apartment properties and in this way is so defrauding the government that at least an investigation is called for. Melissa herself initiates a request with the Federal Reserve Board to have Kraft verify to them and herself that his terms of rental don't exceed the limits of the truth-in-lending law and also that the extra penalties which he attaches to late rental payments don't exceed legal limits for credit billing.

After Melissa finishes these phone calls and her letter writing, she lights a cigarette, smiles, and wonders
how long it will take Mr. Kraft to catch on.

Questions for Your Reflection

1. In spite of her intelligence and education, is Melissa leading a balanced life? Give evidence for your answer.

2. Are there indications that Melissa is being unfair
to herself? How does her fairness or unfairness toward
herself affect her work with other people?

3. Does Melissa seem to recognize her own need to be
loved, her own need to start off relations to all others from
basic respect and seeking the good in them? Why or why
not?

4. How do you explain Melissa's vindictive behavior
toward Mr. Kraft?

5. To what extent have the attitudes and institutions
of white society shaped Melissa into the person she now
is? How would different scenarios have formed her?

6. Under attack by whites, Martin Luther King, Jr.
directed blacks not to allow revenge and violence to cor-
rupt their own hearts, since they *had* to keep believing
that whites, too, belong to the same human family. What
would happen to Melissa if she let King's call to a Christ-
like love and fairness towards persons really touch her?

7. If Melissa refuses respect and fairness to Mr.
Kraft, is she slipping into the same trap of self-degrading
discrimination against which she has been struggling
through her careful writing of successful legal briefs? Explain.

8. Is there evidence that Melissa has so stressed winning a secular education that she's neglected cultivating

her religious life? What seems to be the motivation for Melissa's hard work?

An Experiment

In role playing one tries to take the place of another person in a particular situation and identify the thoughts and feelings of the other personality. In the following brief situations, try to imagine yourself as the person described.

(a) You are a little black boy whose family has just moved into a new neighborhood. You see some children playing down the street and shyly approach to join in the fun. You are just beginning to have a good time when the door opens and an irate woman comes into the yard. She yells at you, "Get out of my yard. No black kid is going to play with my kids!"

(b) You are the only black woman working in a school office with several white women. Part of your duties involves doing clerical work for various faculty members. A professor comes into the office, walks past your desk and asks the clerk at the next desk, "Will you please make fifty copies of this for me?"

(c) You are a Panamanian woman with four young children. You are staying at a shelter for battered women and trying desperately to find housing. When you call in response to ads in the paper, you always mention the fact that you have four children. Several times you have been promised a place, but when you went to see it you were told it was suddenly rented just before you arrived. Then you realize that you have been mistaken for a black woman because your skin is so dark.

(d) You are a young black man just out of college. You were on the dean's list, and with a degree in electronics you felt confident you would get a good job. For six months you have answered every ad in the newspaper and checked out every possible job opening. When you talk to some of your former classmates, you realize that they were hired for the very jobs for which you have been interviewed, even though they were less qualified than you.

Questions for Your Reflection

1. As you tried to identify with each person in the above situations what emotions did you experience? What do these feelings tell you about yourself.
2. Now read each situation again and identify with the white person or persons involved. What feelings do you experience now?
3. Does this experiment bring back to your memory any of your own experiences involving attitudes of racism? How do you view these experiences now?
4. What remedies can you suggest to counteract the subtle attitudes of racism?

GOSPEL EVENT

To grasp Jesus' kind of all-embracing loving-fairness in the following Gospel happening, try to imagine the feelings and sense of distance that a Polish dockworker in Solidarity experiences toward a lieutenant in the Soviet military police. Many factors inclined Jesus to feel this same distance toward a Roman centurion. From boyhood Jesus had lived in a land occupied militarily by the Roman legions. He had heard how cruelly they crucified Jewish rebels. This Roman wasn't a simple soldier but was responsible for a hundred Roman soldiers of the occupation that kept Jesus' people down. Why should Jesus cooperate with an oppressor? And most pertinently, Jesus was convinced that his Father had sent him to heal the "lost sheep of Israel," and not to work with non-Jews.

"When Jesus went into Capernaum a centurion came up and pleaded with him. 'Sir,' he said, 'my servant is lying at home paralyzed, and in great pain.' 'I will come myself and cure him,' said Jesus. The centurion replied, 'Sir, I am not worthy to have you under my roof; just give the word and my servant will be cured. For I am under authority myself, and have soldiers under me; and I say to one man: Go, and he goes, and to another: Come here, and he comes; to my servant: Do this, and he does it.' When Jesus heard this he was astonished and said to those following him, 'I tell you solemnly, nowhere in Israel have I found faith like this. And I tell you that many will come from east and west to take their places with Abraham and Isaac and Jacob at the feast in the kingdom of heaven; but the subjects of the kingdom will be turned into the dark, where there will be weeping and grinding of teeth.' And to the centurion Jesus said, 'Go back, then; you have believed, so let this be done for you.' And the servant was cured at that moment" (Matthew 8:5–13).

Questions for Your Reflection

1. If you were a Polish dockworker whose Solidarity union had been crushed, would you be as open, cooperative and helpful to a lieutenant in the Soviet military police as Jesus was to the Roman centurion in the above incident?

2. Jesus hears the call of the Spirit in the servant's suffering and the centurion's plea. In what similar ways are Christians being called in today's world?

3. His people's popular resentment and disdain of the Romans didn't turn Jesus' love away from this centurion. How do popular attitudes and talk about "our ene-

mies," those foreigners, strangers in the neighborhood, refugees, affect your treatment of all kinds of people?

4. Jesus was "astonished" at the centurion's faith and said that many would come from east and west into the heavenly kingdom. Do you know people who are not Christian but seem to be moving into the heavenly kingdom? Are Christians sometimes as biased toward other Christians as Melissa was toward blacks?

5. How can we follow Jesus in his willingness to serve all kinds of people?

A WORD OF CHRISTIAN WITNESS

The quality of the centurion's faith surprises Jesus. Humanly, it's unusually sensitive and courteous. Knowing that the torah pronounces any Jew defiled who enters the home of a non-Jew, the centurion is considerate of Jesus' reputation. Divinely, the Roman's faith is deep and broad. He penetrates to Jesus' authority and trusts that it will work at a distance at least as well as his own. The fact that Jesus hasn't found such faith yet in all Israel suggests how deeply this centurion has staked his person on Jesus as the one in whom God is visiting this Jewish people.

The response of Jesus to the deep faith of the centurion is an example of God's love. Our English language is so limited in words to express the quality of love. The Greeks have three words for love, and in this way they distinguish sexual love (eros) from the love between friends (philia). The third word "agape" in the Christian sense is reserved for that share in God's love which makes it possible to love all God's family. This love is ever faithful, ever fair. It shares God's energy, and as divine energy working in us, it thrusts forward to affirm and promote every one of God's children—just the way God's own love does, without exclusion. It is too compassionate and strong to be turned off by a sinner, a stranger, an enemy. It is convinced that however people appear to us—quarrelsome, foreign, hostile, traitorous—God now loves each of these persons into life and now calls them into his family forever.

In our tension-racked world, then, this God-like love of one's enemies is an absolute necessity if humanity is to survive. No matter how strange or opposed to us a person may seem, he or she exists as an image of God. Therefore, the only fair thing, the only just thing, to do toward that person is to exercise our gift of God-like love. In fairness, we must affirm energetically that in each human person there is a God-like dignity that deserves unending affirmation and promotion—such as God himself gives that person. Such must be our fundamental posture toward each person. Jesus tells us of his Father, "He makes his sun to shine on good and bad alike" (Matthew 5:45). In like manner we are empowered to have our hearts transformed from living mainly for ourselves into hearts that embrace everyone in the scope of our God-like love, the way Martin Luther King, Jr. did.

A TWENTIETH CENTURY WITNESS

God-like love reaches to all God's children. One of our century's outstanding examples of this all-inclusive love is Rev. Martin Luther King, Jr. His love reached out to ignorant friends, rabid enemies, and even a traitor.

Martin Luther King, Jr. had experienced long hard years of being suspected and opposed. Through those experiences and his reflection on the Gospel he became convinced of the principle of non-violent resistance. With Christ, the non-violent resister, King gradually built up his anti-segregation movement. Just a few days before his death, a militant group of young blacks made him agonize. For he watched these self-styled "Invaders" turn a peaceful demonstration in Memphis into a nightmare of violence. Soon, however, the leader of the Invaders realized how headstrong he and his group had been. His violent initiative had been ill-planned and counterproductive. It was the direct opposite of King's basic principle of non-violent love. This leader came to King and asked forgiveness. From deep in his heart, King found the strength to assert a forgiving love toward this young firebrand and his group.

Earlier, four black children were killed when a church in Birmingham was bombed. How was King to respond to this infamous crime, to this ruthless bias and this murderous brutality? To his stunned and rightly angered people, King spoke heart to heart, "In the spirit of the darkness of this hour, we must not despair, we must not become bitter—we must not lose faith in our *white brothers*." The sign of God-like love is to "maintain the bond of unity." Here King did so even with his oppressors.

At another time, King was told that his home in Montgomery had been bombed. He checked first to see whether his wife, Coretta, and their baby had come through safely. Once assured of this, he next had to face a raging crowd of blacks who demanded retaliation. How did he confront them? Eyeball to eyeball he witnessed to them, "We cannot solve this problem through retaliatory violence. We must meet violence with non-violence. Remember the words of Jesus, "He who lives by the sword will die by the sword." . . . We must love our white brothers no matter what they do to us. We must make them know that we love them . . . . We must meet hate with love."

Volunteers in Dr. King's Birmingham Movement signed a *Commitment Card* which read in part:

72

I HEREBY PLEDGE MYSELF—MY PERSON AND BODY—TO THE NON-VIOLENT MOVEMENT. THEREFORE I WILL KEEP THE FOLLOWING TEN COMMANDMENTS:

1. MEDITATE daily on the teachings and life of Jesus.
2. REMEMBER always that the non-violent movement in Birmingham seeks justice and reconciliation—not victory.
3. WALK and TALK in the manner of love, for God is love.
4. PRAY daily to be used by God in order that all might be free.
5. SACRIFICE personal wishes in order that all might be free.
6. OBSERVE with both friend and foe the ordinary rules of courtesy.
7. SEEK to perform regular service for others and for the world.
8. REFRAIN from the violence of fist, tongue, or heart.
9. STRIVE to be in good spiritual and physical health.
10. FOLLOW the directions of the movement and of the captain on a demonstration.

Questions for Your Reflection

1. Which of these commandments seems hardest for you to keep? Why does this particular commandment seem hardest for you?

2. About the second commandment: why is it a snare and delusion to seek victory more wholeheartedly than justice and reconciliation?

3. Have you found that commandments are helpful to you in making the right choices, in expressing your reverence for God, in serving God more faithfully? Why or why not?

4. Do you believe that the sacrifices needed to communicate, cooperate and maintain unity with others are worth it?

5. Today why are the ordinary rules of courtesy so important?

6. Not harming others is indispensable for moral life. Why isn't it enough for such a life?

7. Suppose you discover that for you "violence of heart" is harder to avoid than is "violence of fist and tongue." What steps can you take to overcome this inner violence?

8. Why is striving for good spiritual and physical health necessary?

9. Should each Christian belong to some movement of his or her choice—whether it be a political, or economic, or cultural or other humanitarian movement? Why or why not?

CALL TO ACTION

1. From King's commandments select the one which you think will most enrich your Christian values and improve your relations with others. Try to incorporate that commandment more fully into your life.

2. Examine your heart to identify the kinds of people you tend to avoid. Pray each day that you might learn to see these people as God sees them.

3. If unconnected with some movement working for

greater fairness, read about several such movements and think seriously of joining one.

4. If you are a member of a movement working for greater justice decide how you can participate more effectively.

7. *Jane, Jake, and Their Four Children*

This Catholic family, of our economy's lower-middle class, live in the Bay Area of California. By much pulling together, Jane and Jake have somehow gotten the three oldest through high school and Jennifer, their youngest, into junior high. Their home, in an old section of Fremont, looks like a house on Archie Bunker's street. Built after World War I, it is neat and modest but there is no indication that Jane and Jake are trying to keep up with the Joneses.

At the nearby GM plant Jake had the job of spraying paint on auto-bodies. He was a good worker and tried to cooperate with the foreman and the other workers. But recently, when GM transferred its auto-body plant to Mexico and laid off 1,200 local workers, Jake also received a pink discharge slip. Luckily, Jane had picked up a job four years earlier as a hospital technician. Her salary is mainly what's keeping the family afloat today, plus Jake's unemployment compensation and a small check from dwindling UAW funds. Now Jake spends his days trying to get odd jobs while looking for a more permanent one. He invests two evenings a week working with people from Bread for the World. On these evenings he either attends their meeting or writes letters to Congresspeople. Sometimes he drives a van that brings one hot meal daily to the elderly poor in the Fremont area.

Two years ago, with her family's approval, Jane had followed her generous heart and responded to the Catholic Relief Service appeal that Americans open their doors to the "boat people" of Southeast Asia. She, Jake and the family had taken in two teenage Vietnamese orphans, victims of the war and its aftermath. The two skinny Vietnamese were slightly older than Jennifer. All the family found them quiet and respectful. The two orphans didn't eat much, worked very hard, learned English surprisingly fast, and helped out around the house and yard. But they did much more for the family. They opened up the family's awareness to Southeast Asia, to the realities of the war, to customs undreamt of, and to so many other things. However, now that Jake's income has been cut so severely, both he and Jane worry how much longer they can host these plucky Vietnamese.

Jane and Jake are faced with another financial problem. At twenty-three, Michael, their oldest son, is thinking seriously of marriage and they would like to help give him a start. Of course, Michael hasn't dared think of purchasing a home. But he would like to lease a three-room apartment and buy some furniture for it. In California, however, rents and furnishings are "out of sight," as Mike found out. The Savings and Loan people are willing to stretch their policy for him a bit and loan him $20,000 at 19%. ("At *only* 19%" was the way they put it.) They called it "unusually good terms for today," considering that Mike is just a high school graduate, with a low income, without much collateral or a permanently employed father. Mike knew that such a loan would probably put him and his fiancée in debt for years. So Mike, Jane and Jake are trying desperately to think of some other solution.

Questions for Your Reflection

1. Do you know personally a family like that of Jane and Jake? Can you identify the various economic pressures on such ordinary people who are doing an outstanding job of rearing their children as good Christians?

2. Have you ever walked the streets and searched the help wanted ads looking for a job? How does this day-after-day failure to find a job affect the psychology of the job-seeker?

3. Do you think that GM, by relocating its plant in Mexico, is in effect pitting Jake against a Mexican paint-sprayer? Do you think that GM should be more responsible for American workers than for workers elsewhere? Why or why not?

4. When a corporation's board of directors is deciding whether to relocate a plant, do you think that greater efficiency should be the determining value that in the end controls their decision? Why or why not?

5. Paul VI and Vatican II teach that a person cannot fulfill his or her "right to develop integrally as a person" unless he or she has an adequate economic base. Does the family of Jane and Jake have such a base now? Does the Mexican paint-sprayer and his family? Does Mike and the family he plans to have? Do the two Vietnamese? Do the poor left in Vietnam, those not lucky enough to escape? Explain the basis for your answer in each case.

6. Does it seem to you that the family of Jane and Jake, as well as the two Vietnamese, look like victims of the competition explosion going on in today's giant multi-national corporations and the two super-powers? Give evidence for your answer.

7. Given the gigantic struggle going on between the two super-powers today, do GM, U.S. Steel, Goodyear, Bank of America and other multi-national corporations

themselves look like victims since all are caught in the competitive battle of "expand or wither," of life or death as corporations? If this competitive battle increases until the year 2000, what results do you realistically predict for ordinary families, for all nations, and for the giant corporations themselves by that date? Explain your answer.

An Experiment

To save us from the sinful forces at work within and around us, Jesus Christ loved us enough to go on an amazing adventure. He actually chose to identify with the simple poor folk of Nazareth for about thirty years. He preferred to live with the poor.

Today the people of God, his Church, have committed themselves to getting into closer contact with the so-called "marginated people." In the experiment this week, can you choose, like Christ, to identify with the poor—not for thirty years as he did, but for about three hours? With Christ, aim to be counter-cultural, at least for a while. For America's mainstream glories in affluence, in the power of being Number One, in feeling strong and secure. So for a while this week, choose to deliberately "swim against this current."

In contacting the economically poor, one needs to remember that America's poorest people are generally ten times better off than at least three-fourths of all the people on our planet. The gap between the "have's" and the "have-not's" keeps increasing as the "have's" tend more and more to separate themselves, physically and psychologically, from the "have-not's." The aim of the experiment this week is to bridge this gap and experience greater solidarity with the poor. Some ways you might do this are:

(a) For several hours help out in an alcoholic drop-in center, or a drug-rehabilitation unit, or a soup-kitchen, or a shelter for battered women.

(b) Join some credible demonstration that is protesting downtown. As you walk and perhaps sing with others against nuclear war, or military aid to Central America, or abortion, notice how you feel under the stares, and maybe slurs, that disagreeing passers-by cast your way.

(c) Invest an afternoon in a home for the elderly. Simply be as psychologically present to them as you can. Listen at heart level to their lives, stories, and concerns.

(d) Phone a day-care center serving economically disadvantaged working mothers and, after arranging to help out for a half-day, work with these women and their children.

(e) Ride the subway or city bus, especially during rush hours. Try to read in the faces of these ordinary people their fears, hopes, desires and basic goodness. Ask yourself whether you really believe that you will be judged on the grounds that whatever you do to these "least little ones" you do to Christ.

Questions for Your Reflection

1. After reflecting privately on the deeper meanings of your personal contact with the poor, letting go those initial passing superficial impressions, share your reflections with the group. After all have shared, try to discover common themes from your varied experiences.

2. If every day you lived like the poor whom you contacted, how would you make out? If you had to budget on less than $4,500 a year for yourself and family, what changes would be forced on you? What kind of food, clothing, housing would you have? Would you have anything left for a telephone, a car, some recreation? How would

you expect to be treated by various welfare officials and the police?

3. Can you remember how often you went to bed at night really pained with hunger? How many of those contacted feel hunger sometime each week?

4. Could it be that in years to come when you're among the elderly, you'll have to scrimp for food and wear only the most ordinary clothes? Do you want more security for yourself than for the people you contacted?

5. Can you identify some factors—local, national, international—that exert this economic pressure on the poor you met? Do the same factors press upon the third world's poor? Do you suppose the third world poor suffer pressures far more severe and dehumanizing? Why or why not?

6. Besides economic pressures, which psychological, political, ethnic, cultural, religious, and commercial pressures on the poor did you detect in your experiment?

7. Did these poor whom you briefly contacted teach you anything about your own life-style? Explain your answer.

GOSPEL EVENT

"There was a rich man who used to dress in purple and fine linen and feast magnificently every day. And at his gate there lay a poor man called Lazarus, covered with sores, who longed to fill himself with the scraps that fell from the rich man's table. Dogs even came and licked his sores. Now the poor man died and was carried away by the angels to the bosom of Abraham. The rich man also died and was buried.

"In his torment in Hades he looked up and saw Abraham a long way off with Lazarus in his bosom. So he cried out, 'Father Abraham, pity me and send Lazarus to dip the tip of his finger in water and cool my tongue, for I am in agony in these flames.' 'My son,' Abraham replied, 'remember that during your life good things came your way, just as bad things came the way of Lazarus. Now he is being comforted here while you are in agony. But that is not all: between us and you a great gulf has been fixed, to stop anyone, if he wanted to, crossing from our side to yours, and to stop any crossing from your side to ours.'

"The rich man replied, 'Father, I beg you then to send Lazarus to my father's house, since I have five brothers, to give them warning so that they do not come to this place of torment too.' 'They have Moses and the prophets,' said Abraham; 'let them listen to them.' 'Ah no, father Abraham,' said the rich man, 'but if someone comes to them from the dead, they will repent.' Then Abraham said to him, 'If they will not listen either to Moses or to the prophets, they will not be convinced even if someone should rise from the dead' " (Luke 16:19–31).

Questions for Your Reflection

1. Do you usually view human work (physical or mental) as the *ordinary* way by which people should support themselves and their families?

2. In the Gospel story do you find Lazarus too sick to do an ordinary full day's work? If so, who should supply him with what he needs to live and develop as a human person?

3. Do you believe it likely that the rich man's luxuries have come entirely from his hard work through the years? Or have they also come from other sources? If so, can you identify other likely sources?

4. Try to identify five or six groups in the U.S. (the world's most affluent country) who are today living like Lazarus. What does the fact that there are such groups tell you?

5. In the whole world today, can you name a half-dozen nations which live like Lazarus?

6. How does our American society take care of its sick, elderly, children, addicts, etc.?

7. Do you think that each American in our economic top 60% is morally obliged in justice to share goods out of his or her abundance with the most afflicted persons in our country and in the world?

8. Does this moral obligation bind in strict justice or is it simply an appeal to kindly hearts? Is it also an urgent obligation in God-given love of our fellow human beings?

9. While paying taxes makes up a large part of this obligatory sharing, do the demands of both strict justice and of Christian love require us to initiate some direct and personal support to the poor?

10. How can Americans who are so busy working and caring for their families become more aware of the suffering people in our slums and in third world nations?

11. To prevent a crippling sense of over-powering guilt it is necessary to identify the sociological factors that force into poverty the lowest 20% of Americans as well as most nations of the third world. What are some of these sociological factors? Do these factors take away all individual guilt? Why or why not?

A WORD OF CHRISTIAN WITNESS

The Gospel story of Lazarus and the rich man teaches a lesson that needs to be stressed today. The rich man of the parable was obliged to give from his useful and superfluous goods enough to keep Lazarus alive and developing positively. The fathers of Vatican Council II are in agreement on this obligation as our world is tending to divide more and more into the "haves" and the "have-nots." They point out that since God created the goods of the world to support *all* his family's members, the exclusiveness of all private property is conditioned and relative to others' needs—whether ordinary or severe or extreme needs. In short, all private property is under a "social mortgage." They put this teaching in a way that deserves quotation in full:

> For the rest, the right to have a share of earthly goods sufficient for oneself and one's family belongs to everyone. The Fathers and Doctors of the Church held this view, teaching that men are obliged to come to the relief of the poor, and to do so not merely out of their superfluous goods. If a person is in extreme necessity, he has the right to take from the riches of others what he himself needs. Since there are so many people in this world afflicted with hunger, this sacred Council urges all, both individuals and government, to remember the saying of the Fathers: "Feed the man dying of hunger, because if you have not fed him, you have killed him." According to their ability, let all individuals and governments undertake a genuine sharing of their goods. Let them use these goods especially to provide individuals and nations with the means for helping and developing themselves ("The Church in the Modern World," #69).

The successors of the apostles gathered at Vatican II gave three reasons for their emphasis on the obligation to help the poor by giving of one's useful goods and luxuries:

1. God intends that the goods of the earth sustain and help all his sons and daughters to live and grow humanly.

2. Every human being is fundamentally equal in having one Creator as his or her common Source, in being empowered by one common, basic, human nature which establishes all as members of the human race, and in looking forward to the same common destiny in the kingdom of God.

3. All human persons are called to take part in the human community's basic processing of goods and services.

One might think that the poor are the only ones who benefit when the rich fulfill their obligation and share their goods. Rather, in this exchange a mutual ministry takes place respecting the different roles of the "have's" and the "have-not's." The poor give to the rich the opportunity of giving generously in a free, prompt and intelligent way. In this giving the rich may come to recognize a certain poverty within themselves—their need to grow in concern for the less fortunate and in compassion. If the rich allow themselves to become ever more preoccupied with the pursuit of material prosperity, they can arrive at a point where they are no longer able to love their fellow human beings. They become such victims of consumerism and affluence that even the minimal requirement of love, to will fairness to all, becomes almost impossible.

On their side, the rich give material aid to the poor and the opportunity for them to develop in a human manner. The poor, by responding with sincere gratitude, have the opportunity to be free from envy and violence toward those who have more. Upon this complex set of attitudes which promote a genuine mutual ministry of poor to rich and rich to poor depends the enhancement of the whole human community. Accordingly, one distinctive mark of a truly healthy society is the effective care of its poor, sick, elderly, handicapped and other disadvantaged members.

Questions for Your Reflection

1. Do you look on yourself as placed by God as his steward over any property he has allowed you to acquire? If so, how did you develop this attitude? If not, what kept you from such a view?

2. Do you believe that all your private property is "under a mortgage to society" so that, in case you didn't use some of it to help those in extreme need, they would have a *strict right* to take enough of your property to keep themselves alive and developing? What would you do if an extremely poor person took some of your property?

3. During the past decades the U.S. Senate has adamantly refused to sign the basic U.N. Covenant on Human Rights and continues to exempt itself from accepting the verdicts of the World Court at the Hague. Does this make the United States look like the rich man in Christ's parable of Lazarus? Why or why not?

4. We hold political candidates publicly accountable for their policies and decisions. Do we hold the directors of our largest corporations publicly accountable to those whose lives are affected by multi-national decisions—American housewives, Central American peasants, Peace Corps volunteers, Church people, all ordinary people? Why has this difference in accountability arisen?

A TWENTIETH CENTURY WITNESS

Some great Catholic women, like Mother Teresa and Dorothy Day, dedicate themselves primarily to the corporal works of mercy. Other great Catholic women, like America's Flannery O'Connor, Sweden's Sigrid Unset, and Germany's Gertrud von le Fort—all imaginative writers of great diversity—show us concretely in their writings how the Christian faith "rises like leaven" within a particular culture.

Barbara Ward belongs generally in this latter group of women who minister to our minds. Yet she was distinctive and extraordinary because she was a *global* as well as an intellectual apostle. Hers was a cosmic consciousness. She raised many minds to that global awareness of "our only earth" which we on our troubled planet need so urgently.

Barbara Ward was born in 1914, received a solid education in both economics and the humanities, and from 1939 served as assistant editor of *The Economist,* England's renowned scrutinizer of business matters. In 1950 she married Sir Robert Jackson, then under-secretary-general of the United Nations. His job took them to India, Pakistan, and Ghana. By living in these places, Barbara Ward Jackson developed her concern for and commitment to the developing countries of the third world. In the last three decades of her life, through lectures, broadcasts, popular essays and a dozen books, she combined her professional skills as an economist with her dazzling gifts for enlightening thought and direct communication to alert the rich of the world to their responsibilities toward the poor and to mobilize people everywhere to preserve the earth we share.

For example, in 1953 Columbia University included in its bicentennial celebration an elaborate conference on education and religion. Among the experts and dignitaries in attendance was Dr. Henry P. Van Dusen, then president of Union Theological Seminary. Van Dusen left the following picture of what happened at that conference when Barbara Ward finally addressed it: "Speaking at the end of two days of talk, which had seemed to many of the participants aggravatingly discursive and unproductive, she delivered virtually ex tempore a 45-minute 'summary' that brought several hundred jaded scholars to their feet in thunderous and prolonged applause. However divided they might have been on the issues in dispute, they were of one mind that this was as brilliant an intellectual and oratorical *tour de force* as any they had ever heard."

But Barbara touched more than scholars. President Lyndon B. Johnson said of her 1962 book, *The Rich Nations and the Poor Nations,* "I read it like I do the Bible."

And at the 1971 Synod of Bishops on world justice, Barbara Ward became the first woman ever to address a synodal session. Her final words witnessed to these bishops the gist of her distinctive message: "Teach us, by word and example, to love and respect this small planet which must carry all humanity. Teach us to moderate our demands, share our resources and seek with all our brothers to make a reality of our prayer, 'Thy kingdom come.' "

In 1976 Queen Elizabeth II gave life peerage to Barbara Ward who thereafter was known officially as Baronness Jackson of Lodsworth, the English town in which she lived and where she died in 1981. Lady Jackson once described the role of the Church: "to make its members into responsible citizens as well as saints." Barbara Ward has, by her life and work, made it easier for the Church to fulfill its role.

To sum up, few people have surpassed Barbara Ward in dedicating their life-energies and gifts to unending research, careful human writing, and widespread dissemination of economic and humanistic ideas. Hers was a humble, intelligent and saintly struggle to overcome the unjust economic structures of our world and to forge fairer ones that will build world peace. She is rightly regarded as a twentieth century symbol of the struggle for that international peace which is the product of justice in its fullness—economic, legal, humanistic and divine.

Questions for Your Reflection

1. Do you think it is important to have a global vision such as Barbara Ward had? If so, how does one acquire this global consciousness?

2. Barbara developed her concern for poor nations of the world by living in several poor countries. What are some other ways of learning compassion for the poor?

3. Why did Barbara think it is so important to "love

and respect this small planet which must carry all humanity"? Concretely, how can this be accomplished?

4. Do you believe that as Americans who make up 6% of the world's population and use 40% of the world's resources we should "moderate our demands and share our resources"? What practical steps are you willing to take in this direction?

CALL TO ACTION

1. Close your left eye, take up a quarter with the thumb and forefinger of your right hand, and then hold it at arm's length in front of your right eye. Move the quarter closer to your eye in four stages, finally completely covering your eye with the quarter. At each stage, notice how many things you are aware of besides the quarter. Reflect on the telltale sense of this parable-in-action.

2. Like Jake, invest some hours each week in an organization that promotes economic justice in a responsibly intelligent way because it uses careful research at the national or international level to guide it—e.g., Bread for the World.

3. Read one of Barbara Ward's short books, e.g., *The Rich Nations and the Poor Nations.*

4. If in your city 80% to 100% of the housing in certain areas is occupied by a minority group, research in your library or other data-center the history and causes of this concentration of a minority group.

5. Write your senator (or phone his local office) to request that he co-sponsor a bill directing the U.S. to endorse the U.N. Covenant of Human Rights and to acknowledge as binding upon itself the verdicts of the World Court of Justice at the Hague.

8. *Bill and Sue*

Bill has been working for BBT Electronics for eighteen years. The company began as a small business that made components for larger industries. Over the years the business has grown through its reputation for making precision parts. Just last year the company was awarded a government contract. At first the workers at the plant did not know what they were making. Gradually the rumor spread that the tiny, intricate relay was part of a system for a new nuclear weapon, more powerful than anything now in existence.

Bill was very upset when he heard the rumor. It bothered him that he was helping to build a weapon that could wipe out whole cities and their surrounding countrysides. Bill talked to several of his friends and discovered that some of them felt the same way he did. It made him feel better that he was not alone but it didn't solve the problem. Bill said to Dick, "As I see it, we're really in a bind. I don't like working on anything that goes into a nuclear weapon but I can't quit either. I've got three kids who are still in school. Besides I can't risk losing my pension." Dick understood. He had four small children and he knew how hard it was to find a job to support them. They had heard of workers in other plants quitting their jobs when the company became involved in nuclear weapons. They wished they could do the same. They admired these men and they felt guilty for not standing up for their convictions.

When Bill and Dick saw the nonchalant way their fellow workers were acting they began to doubt their own convictions. After all, they weren't responsible for getting the contract. They weren't responsible for the way the products they made were used. If their plant did not make the relays, some other company would, so why worry? Gradually Bill and Dick began to put their concerns out of their minds but somehow they didn't feel the same about their jobs. Bill began counting the months until he could retire, but Dick had many working years ahead of him. Dick tried to look for another job, but working every day didn't leave him much time for job hunting. He promised himself he would spend his next vacation checking into other job opportunities.

Last week when Bill came home from work, his wife Sue seemed thoughtful, but excited too. She had heard that their parish was considering offering sanctuary to a Salvadoran family. Bill said, "You'd better be careful, Sue. I think it's illegal to help undocumented aliens."

"But, Bill, the Church has always granted sanctuary to those who are fleeing from persecution. In the last three years more than 40,000 civilians have been killed in El Salvador. These people have good reason to fear for their lives."

"Well, you'd better find out more about the legal implications before you get involved. I just read that two people were arrested in Texas for transporting three Salvadoran refugees."

The following week Sue attended a meeting where a woman lawyer tried to explain to the group the risk they might be taking. It was all very confusing. According to the U.N. Protocol and the U.S. Refugee Act, Central Americans fleeing persecution are lawfully present in the

United States. It seemed that the whole problem hinged on whether the person has a "well-founded fear of persecution on account of race, religion, nationality, membership in a particular social group or political opinion." The lawyer scared Sue when she said, "In spite of the fact that the U.S. signed the U.N. Protocol, criminal charges can be brought against you for harboring or transporting refugees. U.S. officials do not want to believe that Salvadorans have a 'well-founded fear of persecution.' It contradicts their Central American policy." Sue left the meeting feeling very sad.

Questions for Your Reflection

1. Do you feel that Bill and Dick are too conscientious being concerned about the use of the products they are helping to manufacture?

2. Have you ever been in a similar situation? If you have, can you share with the group how you felt?

3. If Bill and Dick came to you for advice, what would you tell them?

4. Are there other jobs that present similar problems to workers? What suggestions do you have for solving these problems?

5. Is it patriotic to question the decisions of the U.S. government? Explain your answer.

6. What risk is Sue taking if she becomes involved in the sanctuary movement? If you were in Sue's place, what would you do?

7. Are there situations where one's faith in Jesus and his message seem to demand acts of civil disobedience? Give some examples.

8. What criteria would you use to decide when civil disobedience is in order?

An Experiment

1. Prepare a list of government actions that you have disagreed with. Evaluate your reactions in each case. On what was your opposition based?

2. The term "unjust structure" is used to describe the manner of systematic operation by governments or large organizations which is unjust to groups of people, often the poor or ethnic groups. Look at some structures with which you are familiar, for example, our system of taxation, welfare, our judicial system, etc., and identify any injustices you find in the system. Who are the people who suffer from these injustices?

3. Ask a minister in some inner-city parish to put you in contact with someone who has to apply for food stamps. Then accompany that person as he or she moves through the mazes of officialdom to secure his or her food stamps. Ask yourself while taking these steps, what message these bureaucrats actually, even if unintentionally, convey.

GOSPEL EVENT

"They then led Jesus from the house of Caiaphas to the praetorium. It was now morning. They did not go into the praetorium themselves or they would be defiled and unable to eat the passover. Pilate came outside to them and said, 'What charge do you bring against this man?' They replied, 'If he were not a criminal, we should not be handing him over to you.' Pilate said, 'Take him yourselves, and try him by your own law.' The Jews answered, 'We are not allowed to put a man to death.' This was to fulfill the words Jesus had spoken indicating the way he was going to die.

"So Pilate went back into the praetorium and called Jesus to him. 'Are you the king of the Jews?' he asked. Jesus replied, 'Do you ask this of your own accord, or have others spoken to you about me?' Pilate answered, 'Am I a Jew? It is your own people and the chief priests who have handed you over to me. What have you done?' Jesus replied, 'Mine is not a kingdom of this world; if my kingdom were of this world, my men would have fought to prevent my being surrendered to the Jews. But my kingdom is not of this kind.' 'So you are a king then?' said Pilate. 'It is you who say it,' answered Jesus. 'Yes, I am a king. I was born for this, I came into the world for this: to bear witness to the truth; and all who are on the side of truth listen to my voice.' 'Truth?' said Pilate. 'What is that?' And with that he went out again to the Jews and said, 'I find no case against him. But according to a custom of yours I should release one prisoner at the Passover; would you like me, then, to release the king of the Jews?' At this they shouted: 'Not this man,' they said, 'but Barabbas.' Barabbas was a brigand.

"Pilate then had Jesus taken away and scourged; and after this, the soldiers twisted some thorns into a crown and put it on his head, and dressed him in a purple robe. They kept coming up to him and saying, 'Hail, king of the Jews,' and they slapped him in the face.

"Pilate came outside again and said to them, 'Look, I am going to bring him out to you to let you see that I find no case.' Jesus then came out wearing the crown of thorns and the purple robe. Pilate said, 'Here is the man.' When they saw him the chief priests and the guards shouted, 'Crucify him! Crucify him!' Pilate said, 'Take him yourselves and crucify him. I can find no case against him.' 'We have a law,' the Jews replied 'and according to that law he ought to die, because he has claimed to be the Son of God.'

"When Pilate heard them say this his fears increased. Re-entering the praetorium, he said to Jesus, 'Where do you come from?' But Jesus made no answer. Pilate then said to him, 'Are you refusing to speak to me? Surely you know I have power to release you and I have power to crucify you?' 'You would have no power over me,' replied Jesus, 'if it had not been given you from above; that is why the one who handed me over to you has the greater guilt.'

"From that moment Pilate was anxious to set him free, but the Jews shouted, 'If you set him free you are no friend of Caesar's; anyone who makes himself king is defying Caesar.' Hearing these words, Pilate had Jesus brought out, and seated himself on the chair of judgment at a place called the Pavement, in Hebrew Gabbatha. It was Passover Preparation Day, about the sixth hour. 'Here is your king,' said Pilate to the Jews. 'Take him away, take him away!' they said. 'Crucify him!' 'Do you want me to crucify your king?' said Pilate. The chief priests answered, 'We have no king except Caesar.' So in the end Pilate handed him over to them to be crucified" (John 18:28—19:16).

Questions for Your Reflection

1. What was Pilate's attitude toward Jesus? Did he consider him an equal human person or someone he could dominate and use to keep the city peaceful during the festival time? What actions or omissions by Pilate support your answer?

2. What are the dangers that arise when government officials treat people *primarily* as things rather than *primarily* as free and equal persons whose overall good is to be promoted by the government?

3. In the Nicene Creed that the Church recites each Sunday, the only human person mentioned explicitly, besides Mary, is Pilate—"crucified under Pontius Pilate." As you say these words has it occurred to you that Christ in his mystical body is still suffering from the tactics of peo-

ple like Pilate? Give some examples you have noticed recently.

A WORD OF CHRISTIAN WITNESS

It is possible in thinking of government to become so caught up in organizational structures—the branches of government, departments, cabinet posts, committees, etc.—that one loses sight of the purpose of government. The principal function of government is to promote the common good. The common good refers to the growing condition of society in which individual citizens can more easily exercise their rights and fulfill their duties.

A number of Church documents, among them *Mater et Magistra* and *Pacem in Terris,* have dealt with the function of government in some detail. Pope John XXIII stated: "It is agreed that in our time the common good is chiefly guaranteed when personal rights and duties are maintained. The chief concern of civil authorities must therefore be to insure that these rights are acknowledged, respected, coordinated with other rights, defended and promoted, so that in this way each one may more easily carry out his duties. . . . One of the fundamental duties of civil authorities, therefore, is so to coordinate and regulate social relations that the exercise of one man's rights does not threaten others in the exercise of their own rights nor hinder them in the fulfillment of their duties. Finally, the rights of all should be effectively safeguarded and, if they have been violated, completely restored" (*Pacem in Terris,* #60, 62).

The Church documents also point out that since government exists for the common good it must foster the production of a sufficient supply of material goods. Developments in science and technology now make it possible for public authorities to lessen the gap between the very rich and the very poor. They also have it in their power to reduce the economic imbalance between different sectors of the United States and even between different nations in the world. In other words, government has the obligation to strive for the economic good of all peoples, even on a worldwide scale. It seems fairly obvious that the obligation to safeguard the rights of citizens includes the economic rights of all, especially workers, women, children, elderly and the poor of all ages. In general, government must show special care for those who cannot protect their own rights.

In its relationship with individuals and small groups government must walk a fine line. Individuals and small groups must have the freedom to act autonomously in their dealings and cooperation with one another. Still they must be aware of their obligation to the common good. When individuals and groups neglect this obligation, then government must step in skillfully to regulate the activity.

The dignity of the human person includes the right to take an active part in the affairs of state. This is not a right bestowed by the state but a right inherent in the human nature of the person. Therefore, the state cannot deprive people of their rights for any length of time. In case of an emergency, the state may curtail the exercise of certain rights but only for the good of all citizens. Civil authorities must then make strenuous efforts to restore the condition of society where the individual citizens can exercise their rights and fulfill their duties.

Although great emphasis has been put on respect for the law in the United States, we cannot deny the fact that the earliest settlers were dissenters. They came to the New World to be free from Old World restraints that violated their rights. Throughout our history there have been individuals and groups who responded to the dictates of conscience and engaged in civil disobedience.

Henry David Thoreau's essay, popularly known as "Civil Disobedience," advocates non-compliance with unjust law as a way of making a public statement calling attention to the need for reform of the structures supporting the evil. That civil disobedience can be very effective in changing unjust structures is evidenced by Gandhi's nonviolent resistance to the oppressive British occupation of India. Gandhi led a mass-movement of Indians protesting the unjust structures which the British were imposing on them—tax on salt, regulation of textile-imports, curtailing participation in governmental decisions, etc. More recently conscientious Americans saw the need of civil disobedience to alert their fellow Americans to their belief that increasing military fire-power against the Vietnamese was an immoral step.

In the case of Bill, his conscience might tell him that he can no longer be involved in producing weapons that could kill millions of fellow human beings. Even if these weapons are never used, they are already killing people. Money that could feed a starving world, that could provide jobs for the unemployed, is being channeled into more and more devastating weapons. If Bill quits his job, he has done a very courageous thing but he is not disobedient to the law. On the other hand, if he takes direct action against the plant, he is engaging in civil disobedience and must be ready to accept the consequences.

If Sue feels called to help provide sanctuary for the refugees in her parish, there are several questions she should ask herself:

(a) Why do I feel I am called to do this?
(b) Do I have enough information to make an intelligent choice?
(c) Have I talked it over with other people whose lives could be affected by my choice?
(d) Are there other ways of highlighting the unjust policy of our government?

(e) What are the legal implications?

(f) Can I sustain, physically and psychologically, the possible consequences of my action?

Questions for Your Reflection

1. Make a list of your rights and duties as a citizen. Do you feel that you are deprived of any of your rights or hindered in fulfilling your duties? Which ones?

2. Are there any non-violent ways you could claim your rights? What are they?

3. Have you ever been called to take a stand in civil disobedience? What was the result for you? for your family? for your friends?

A TWENTIETH CENTURY WITNESS

In 1892, there was born, in Breslau (now Wroclaw in Poland) of Jewish parents, a child who may be seen as a symbol of all those who suffer from unjust governmental action. Edith Stein was an exceptionally intelligent child whose inquisitive mind led her to abandon her Jewish faith and become an agnostic while still in secondary school. Her intense desire to know the truth led her to the study of philosophy.

Her studies were interrupted by World War I. She served her country as a nursing aide for the Red Cross. As soon as the war was over she resumed her studies in Germany under the leading philosophers of the time. Edmund Husserl, the famous philosopher, recognized in Edith the best student he had ever known. She became his assistant and began her career as a professional philosopher, writer and teacher. During this time she continued her personal search for life's meaning and gradually moved toward Christianity. The turning point of her conversion came when she read the autobiography of Therese of Lisieux. She was so gripped by Therese's story that she read the whole book in one night. As she finished the next morning she said, "This is truth," and promptly became a Catholic.

As the Nazis came to power in Germany, Edith was deprived of her teaching post because she was a Jew. For some time she had desired to become a Carmelite but was persuaded that her teaching, lecturing and philosophical writing were influencing so many people for good that she should not give them up. Now that she could no longer teach and lecture, she entered Carmel in Cologne in October 1933 at the age of forty-two.

The Nazis persecution of the Jews became more intense and Edith's presence in the Carmel of Cologne was a danger to all the nuns. She was transferred to Echt in Holland with her sister Rosa. They felt safe in Holland until the Nazis invaded Holland.

In July 1942 the Dutch bishops issued a pastoral letter denouncing Nazi persecution of the Jews. In retaliation, the Gestapo rounded up one thousand Jewish Catholics, among them Edith and her sister. On August 2 Edith and Rosa were arrested and put on the train for Auschwitz. That very day Edith had finished her book, *The Science of the Cross*. Her final words are a note she smuggled out of Auschwitz before she was led naked to the gas chamber on August 9. The note read, "One can only learn the 'Science of the Cross' if one feels the Cross in one's own person. I was convinced of this from the very first and have said it with all my heart. 'Hail the Cross, our only hope.' "

Questions for Your Reflection

1. In what ways can Edith Stein be considered a symbol of all those who suffer from governmental injustice?

2. Edith fled from Germany to Holland to escape arrest. Is this a Christian response? Why or why not?

3. Have you ever experienced unjust treatment from government officials? How did you react?

4. Do you agree with Edith that the Cross is our only hope against the injustices of today? Explain your answer.

CALL TO ACTION

As a result of your reflections on this chapter, what positive step will you take during the coming week to counteract an unjust situation?

9. Ramona, Bob and Their Three Children

With snow still on his boots, ten year old Jimmy leads his family into the house after their return from the 10 A.M. Sunday Mass. "He did it again!" cries Jimmy, stomping the snow from his boots. "Monsignor talked about money *again*! I'll bet he's done that for fifteen out of the last twenty Sundays." Home from college on a brief break, Jimmy's older brother Terry joins in, "Yeah, and the rare times he doesn't preach money he talks off the cuff." Meanwhile, Ramona is already in the kitchen preparing Sunday brunch for her family with the somewhat reluctant help of Kathy, her high school sophomore daughter.

During the wait, her husband Bob flips on the TV and samples the various evangelists doing their thing this Sunday morning. For a while he watches a well-dressed preacher holding forth in luxurious surroundings. Amid the luminous splendor of prosperity, the preacher soothingly tells his audience how to maintain peace of soul. Only in passing does he refer to Jesus and salvation. Never does he mention that Christians have the difficult job of witnessing Christ's challenging truth and example to unbelievers and skeptics. Never does he tell his audience that they must enter the political forum and witness to others the mind of Christ on nuclear arms, racism, and sexism. He certainly does not convey to them Christ's mind on the difficulty a rich man has to enter the kingdom of God. Annoyed by the one-sided Gospel being preached without any of Christ's challenge, Bob flips to another channel doing a replay of the President's meet-the-press conference last night. With nonchalant humor, the President skirts a tough question about the mounting federal deficit. Beaming complete confidence, he reassures a hesitant woman-reporter that $300 billion is a minimum for next year's defense budget. Then, when the strains of his favorite martial air fill the room, he smiles, waves to his audience and marches from the podium.

The next evening, when the family gathers around the dinner table, young Kathy recounts her day at Roosevelt High. She shares her worry about tomorrow's history exam that she has to cram for. The only thing her teacher demands is detailed facts. He never asks his history students for essays that would call them to link the facts together and weave them into a meaningful basic message from the past.

Kathy's lament prompts Terry to report on his last week at the university. His literature prof simply evokes student discussion on the pros and cons of Hemingway's various accounts of extramarital relations. The prof never presents either his own position or any reasons that might lead to it. Terry sums up his overall experience thus far in business college as feeling pushed into society's elite, upwardly mobile class. He has also been cautioned against a certain midwestern conservatism that tends to overlook the rare opportunities to amass a fortune and to enjoy the privileges that go with it. Terry's mother asks him whether he can make it into this jet-set without stepping on people. Looking at her in puzzlement, Terry wonders how his mother's attitude and feelings can be so different from those of his teachers and business school classmates. Then he remembers that his mother even enjoys helping the poor and elderly on her Wednesday afternoons at the low-cost housing unit. She's a paradox to him.

During dessert, Terry mentions that recently on TV he saw a wireless phone-set advertised for less than $200, including installation of the base-unit. That would really help him while he is doing his lawn work during the summer. He could keep in touch with all his friends. Meanwhile, Kathy notices the new trend in the conversation and doesn't want to miss an opportunity. She loves to sun and lounge at the edge of a pool and drop in periodically to cool off. So she soon blurts out that a wonderful way to beat the sizzling heat predicted for this summer would be to install in their own backyard that octagonal swimming pool she saw advertised for only $3,500. Both Bob and Ramona swallow hard on that one—a pause that only makes room for Jimmy to pipe in, "For my bithday this June, I need a 15-speed bike that'll help me up the hills at camp this summer. It's only $450. And since Terry and Kathy got their hi-fi's on their birthdays, why shouldn't I get my own portable one so that I can take it to camp?" His dad asks Jim where he spotted the ad for this 15-speed bike. Jimmy tells of being over at the neighbor's house two doors away with a gang of older fellows. They were watching basketball on regular TV and shows on cable and the bike ad came in there somewhere. When his mother inquires which programs they were watching on cable, Jimmy's face turns red as he mumbles something about Dracula and "weirdo love shows." Then, suddenly announcing that he'd better get to his job of shoveling the snow before he does his studies, he exits quickly from the dining room.

Questions for Your Reflection

1. A persuasion system works in our culture to influence people to think or behave in a certain way. Can you

identify four or five persuasion systems influencing Ramona, Bob and their three children?

2. As you detect the kind of school or group that is shaping Terry, Kathy and Jimmy, respectively, which unfair structures do you find at work in those persuasion systems?

3. How do you detect whether a priest or minister is conveying the *full* Gospel of Christ or only his self-serving version of it?

4. After hearing a genuinely helpful homily, do you sometimes thank the minister? After a series of poor homilies have you taken prudent steps, individually or in a group, to suggest ways of improving his or her ministry?

5. Is Kathy's history teacher unfair to Kathy and the class by his style of teaching? Give reasons for your answer.

6. What is consumerism? Are the children victims of it? Explain your answer.

7. Just how much influence on yourself and your children is being exercised by: (a) schools? (b) TV, radio, newspapers, magazines, movies and popular songs? (c) politicians and government? (d) church people? After your group shares its answers, discuss what positive steps you can take to challenge these persuasion systems to a fairer, more responsible service. Discuss what steps you need to take if you are effectively to counteract half-truths, misleading slogans, and other unfair communications that are broadcast.

An Experiment

Do one of the following this week and report back to your group.

1. Leaf through a magazine or newspaper to discover and clip three ads which seem to you to actually mislead the ordinary reader. The Better Business Bureau gener-

ally monitors all ads closely and approves about 95% of them. How do the standards of your group differ from those of the Better Business Bureau?

2. Investigate what's behind Jimmy's blush and his mumbling about "weirdo love stories." Talk to a teacher from junior high and check whether almost all seventh graders have viewed a pornographic movie on cable TV. Report your findings to the group and discuss ways of counteracting this unjust system which crushes Christian youngsters' native sense of modesty and reverence toward the human body as a temple of the Holy Spirit.

3. Contrast how frequently the media highlights (a) the danger of smog, acid rain, and pollution with (b) how often they publicly examine their own responsibility for their hour-after-hour showing of violence, sexual looseness and disregard for the dignity of the human person. Decide on one or two ways of claiming your rights as a TV viewer not to be manipulated by the media.

GOSPEL EVENT

"The kingdom of heaven is like this. A man sowed his field with good seed; but while everyone was asleep his enemy came, sowed darnel (weeds) among the wheat, and made off. When the wheat sprouted and began to fill out, the darnel could be seen among it. The farmer's men went to their master and said, 'Sir, was it not good seed that you sowed in your field? Then where has the darnel come from?' 'This is an enemy's doing,' he replied. 'Well then,' they said, 'shall we go and gather the darnel?' 'No,' he answered; 'in gathering it you might pull up the wheat at the same time. Let them both grow together till harvest; and at harvest-time I will tell the reapers, "Gather the darnel first, and tie it in bundles for burning; then collect the wheat into my barn."' . . .

"Jesus then dismissed the people, and went into the house, where his disciples came to him and said, 'Explain to us the parable of the darnel in the field.' And this was his answer: 'The sower of the good seed is the Son of Man. The field is the world; the good seed stands for the children of the kingdom, the darnel for the children of the evil one. The enemy who sowed the darnel is the devil. The harvest is the end of time. The reapers are the angels. As the darnel, then, is gathered up and burnt, so at the end of time the Son of Man will send out his angels, who will gather out of his kingdom whatever makes men stumble, and all whose deeds are evil, and these will be thrown into the blazing furnace, the place of wailing and grinding of teeth. And then the righteous will shine as brightly as the sun in the kingdom of their Father. If you have ears, then hear' " (Matthew 13:24–30, 36–43).

Questions for Your Reflection

1. Since Jesus called himself the "truth" and the "light of the world," what responsibility for communicating the truth frankly and openly to others do his disciples have?

2. If Christ calls the enemy, the devil, the "father of lies," what will be the mark of the devil's influence in our lives? In the lives of those around us?

3. Does the fact that there is evil as well as good in the world help us to become better Christians? Explain.

4. Amid our continuing battle against half-truths, misinformation and unfair stereotypes, which attitudes do we need to find the truth to live by?

5. Can you identify some ways in which churches, schools, mass media and political officials function as sowers of "good seed"? as sowers of "bad seed"?

6. In what ways do you see yourself as also a mixture of wheat and weed?

A WORD OF CHRISTIAN WITNESS

The quality of life in interpersonal relationships and in society at large depends on how fully truth is communicated. A truthful person speaks the truth, without understating or overstating it, neither distorting, nor pretending, nor bluffing. Such a person communicates truth with compassion, always careful not to harm another's reputation. An individual of this kind is one who can be relied upon, one who has the ability to become a trustworthy friend.

Beyond the level of interpersonal relationships, Americans are immersed in educational systems, in a flood of newsprint, magazines, latest musical hits, movies, radio and TV, in the rhetoric of politicians, and the various messages of church ministers. Since truth in communications is so vital between individuals, how much more important is it when systems of communication are involved. These systems of persuasion magnify by thousands or millions of times the power to communicate either for good or evil. John F. Kennedy recognized the power of these communication systems and pleaded with media personnel to respect every person's right to a truly balanced, ever more adequate account of the news.

Although basically good, this enlarged power is unfortunately used too often to spread misinformation or half-truths in self-serving ways. Instead of being aimed at the good of all people, these systems then become directed to maintain certain persons in power or to fashion someone's image this way rather than that. They may claim to be presenting nothing but the facts yet never mention that their facts are carefully selected to support a particular view.

Americans are rightly concerned about the ill effects that drugs are inflicting on the physical and psychological health of our youth. Of even deeper concern should be the ill effects that half-truths, slanted approaches, and blind guides are inflicting upon the minds and hearts of adults and especially of children.

Most governments in the world have no doubt about the mammoth power of communications media. They immediately reach out to control TV, radio, newspapers, schools, and even churches. For if through a broadcast their citizens were to discover a fuller truth, radical changes would follow in public opinion, and thus in government, and maybe even in the economic or cultural structure of the country.

The communist governments (second world countries) keep strictest watch that nothing but the "party line" is carried by their persuasion systems. They deal sharply with vocal dissidents. Today the United States, western Europe and Japan (first world countries) dominate in communications systems through computer research, communication satellites and the most heavily used news agencies, e.g., Associated Press, United Press, and Reuters. Here the first world is in such a dominant position that at the United Nations the many developing nations of the third world are, with some legitimacy, demanding a New International Information Order. This new order would require editorial boards of networks and newspapers to be less slanted in favor of the first world and also to reflect the situation and interests of the overlooked three-fourths of the earth's population.

In many third world countries, meanwhile, high percentages of people are trapped in illiteracy. Hence, the media's skillfully arranged sights and sounds easily dupe them with its propaganda. A case in point is Nestle's scandalous early campaign that used vans with loudspeakers to persuade mothers to buy Nestle's infant milk formula even though the villages' impure water would contaminate the milk in the mixing. Yet it is not enough to be raised to literacy. Unless people are trained to view ads critically they will continue to be fooled by the catchy tune, the snappy slogan or beautiful picture produced by the ad industries. Certain industries prey upon the young, the illiterate, and the uncritical.

There are other ways that massively warped persuasion systems keep the full truth from people. Some newspapers and journals pander to the sensational in order to sell. Adult movies and magazines promote eroticism and voyeurism to make money. Mass media regard profit from their ad accounts with big corporations as more important than the public's need for more balanced and more adequate truth. Motivated by the desire for greater profits they lack the practical commitment to present accounts that are not only tasteful and telling, but also more adequately balanced and true. Slanted TV, radio and newspaper reporting is a classic example of an unjust societal structure.

This unfair use of power can be reformed. Media people can commit themselves, personally and as a group, to channel the truth in the way which best serves the public's need for the full story. They can also invite some responsible non-media people to serve on monitor boards that periodically offer their verdict to the public on the performance of a particular media. Of course, anyone coming to America from communist or socialist regimes should, for good reasons, admire our free press tradition in all our media. Yet most media people with experience here will easily point out the many restraints that still hinder fully truthful communication by the media to the American public.

Questions for Your Reflection

1. Do you experience that communications media are doing about as good a job as can be expected in presenting

in-depth news reports that are fully balanced and multi-sided? What cases can you cite?

2. Since you cannot completely seal off your children from TV, radio, movies, popular songs and magazines, and thus cannot keep them from some of the weed-sowing by the evil one of which the Gospel speaks, how do you educate their sense of discernment so that they can reject what is evil and embrace what is good?

3. Can you predict what would happen to our news programs if the major networks had to have their editorial boards composed of as many citizens of second and third world countries as there are first world members on them? Explain your prediction.

4. How does the business of manufacturing cars differ from the business of manufacturing news? How should the attitudes of the executive directors reflect this difference?

5. If you are not satisfied with the school system in your area, have you taken part in a P.T.A. meeting in order to voice your requests for better schooling? If so, share your experience with the group. If not, share your other initiatives taken to improve our schools.

6. Sometimes persuasion systems operate on the inadequate idea that justice is the power of the stronger. What is the basis of justice which this inadequate idea fails to respect?

A TWENTIETH CENTURY WITNESS

Dag Hammarskjold, the future international civil servant, was born in Sweden in 1905 and was educated in political science and economics. Unmarried, he chose to become assistant professor of political economics at Stockholm University in 1933. Less than two decades later he was chosen to serve as Sweden's undersecretary of state and soon as minister of state. During these years he became known at the United Nations as Sweden's delegate to the General Assembly. In 1953 he was elected as the general secretary of the United Nations and was reelected to this post in 1957. He spent himself on countless missions to the Near East, to Peking, to the Congo, trying to maintain and enhance peace between nations. His Christian reflections, published under the title of *Markings,* allow a reader to see how much commitment to Christ and to the way of the Cross filled the heart of this unobtrusive, dedicated servant of world peace.

We can take his following words as if spoken to persons who design and manage persuasion systems, people who are tempted to use the medium and message to get their audience to think as newsmakers want people to think. Dag Hammarskjold finds a fundamentally un-Christian disrespect of persons as persons in those yielding to this temptation. He writes of "Jesus' 'lack of principles.' He sat at meal with publicans and sinners, he consorted with harlots. Did he do this to obtain their votes? Or did he think that perhaps he could convert them by such 'appeasement'? Or was his humanity rich and deep enough to make contact, even in them, with that in human nature which is common to all men, indestructible, and upon which the future has to be built?"

Questions for Your Reflection

1. How did Dag Hammarskjold use his power as general secretary of the United Nations?

2. Although you may not have a powerful position can you influence others for good? How is influence different from manipulation of others?

3. Do you agree with Dag Hammarskjold's view of Jesus as he related to publicans and sinners? Why or why not?

1. Pay a well-prepared visit to a local TV program director. Discuss with him or her the steps needed to improve the level of TV programming in your city.

2. Attach a label marked "Voting Booth" near the control knob of your TV set. Practice voting "No, not good enough!" by either switching to another channel or turning the set off completely. Keep tab for a month of your voting record and send a tally of it to your TV program director. Thank the director for the best shows and mention which programs received a "No" vote from you and why.

3. Form a civic monitor group with several other people. For three or four months monitor a local TV station or newspaper. Keep track of editorial directions, headlines or catch phrases, kinds and amounts of violence that were broadcast. Do the same with some highly reputable medium (e.g., PBS, *The Christian Science Monitor*) as a control. Then not only report your findings to the editor involved but also publish your report.

4. Ask your teenagers to read the parable of the wheat and the weeds and join with you in prayerful reflection on it. Then dialogue with them on the struggle they experience from the hidden persuaders opposed to Christian values.

10. St. Michael's Parish

St. Michael's Parish recently celebrated its centenary. For a hundred years immigrant Irish families have invested their play and labors, their joys and sorrows into building this Roman Catholic community. With affection and faith they have reared their children and built their parish church. Their church stands as a monument of their century-old community life in this country, a showplace of which they are deservedly proud.

They celebrated their centenary ten years after the close of Vatican II. Their exceptional, far-seeing pastor, Fr. John, had used those ten years well. Knowing that his own years were numbered, he enlisted the cooperation of his parishioners, sisters and assistants to create a local community that would serve as a model of a post-Vatican II local church.

Father John and his dedicated assistants so won the hearts of his parishioners that even the professional people in the parish—the accountants, lawyers, and doctors—invested their efforts in the community. Fr. John knew that these professional people were too tightly scheduled to plan Sunday liturgies regularly, but they did have some hours each week. So they came at odd hours, either to keep the books or count the collection or prepare notices for the bulletin, and even to clean the church. Moreover, the ingenious choir director achieved a difficult balancing act. He trained the entire congregation to enter into the people's songs during the Mass and yet saved a fitting role for his exceptional choir. Meanwhile, the sisters had trained the lectors to proclaim the word of God with reverence and clarity.

But St. Michael's wasn't a liturgy-only parish. Canada's gift to the parish, a group of five Grey Nuns, stimulated and helped organize the parishioners for action during the week. After a few years, there were hospitality committees welcoming newcomers to the parish, outreach programs for the elderly, divorced, teenagers and catechumens. The flourishing CCD program employed twenty-four licensed instructors who took refresher courses periodically to maintain their licenses. Then, without warning, Fr. John died.

Appointed as new pastor of St. Michael's was a vigorous, energetic Irish priest, dedicated to bringing back the old traditions. His claim was that the cardinal had sent him to St. Michael's to curb the excesses and to bring the parish back to proper order. Within two weeks of his arrival, he had disbanded the parish council, discontinued the lay collection-counters, and forbidden altar girls in the sanctuary. All Communion ministers were to be male. Women lectors were no longer allowed to read at Mass, not even the sisters. Meanwhile, he removed the bright banners hanging in the church. As for participation at Mass he ordered missalettes for everybody. The result was that the congregation no longer concentrated on listening to the word of God being proclaimed, but buried their heads in the pages, if they held the booklets at all.

Of course, this new pastor made all these moves the way a classic autocratic pastor of nineteenth century rural Ireland would have done. He consulted with no one for any of these moves, not even with his assistants and certainly not with the sisters nor with the previously elected members of the now disbanded parish council.

After he had the parish back in order he began taking

off three days each week to rest on the Cape or visit with friends. Meanwhile, he kept his assistants on a tight schedule, allowing them only a half-day off per week. Besides offering a daily parish Mass, they had to make morning trips to distribute Communion to the elderly people of the parish. They still had their five classes of religion in the nearby diocesan high school and in the evenings had to take over the newly organized Baltimore Catechism classes or supervise the Wednesday night bingo game in the parish hall. They still tried to prepare their Sunday homilies but were so busy with other duties that they had less and less time. They noticed that the pastor nearly always had something to say about money during his homilies but they made up their minds not to fall into that trap.

Questions for Your Reflection

1. If you visited St. Michael's one year after the arrival of the new pastor, what feelings would you find among the parishioners? What unjust actions would you expect them to mention as the basis for these feelings?

2. Would you recommend that they simply bide their time, be patient? Do you see other ways open to them?

3. Would you take your children out of St. Michael's new CCD program? Why or why not?

4. When drafting the U.S. Constitution, our founding fathers inserted checks and balances to prevent any one person from gaining control over decisions and finance. Does the local parish have similar checks and balances to prevent grabbing of power in the parish?

5. How does seminary formation and the ordinary life of a parish assistant influence a priest's behavior when he becomes a pastor?

6. If St. Michael's assistant priests endure their new pastor for five or more years, do you predict that when

they are made pastors they too will want to control the decision making and finances of their parishes? Give reasons for your answer.

An Experiment

Examine carefully the following directives issued by the World Synod of Bishops, gathered in Rome in 1971 to treat of justice.

Within the Church, rights must be preserved. No one should be deprived of his ordinary rights because he is associated with the Church in one way or another. Those who serve the Church by their labor, including priests and religious, should receive a sufficient livelihood and enjoy the social security which is customary in their region. Lay people should be given fair wages and a system of promotion. We reiterate the recommendations that lay people should exercise more important functions with regard to Church property and should share in its administration.

We also urge that women should have their own share of responsibility and participation in the community life of society and likewise of the Church. We propose that this matter be subjected to a serious study employing adequate means: for instance, a mixed commission of men and women, religious and lay people of differing situations and competence.

The Church recognizes everyone's right to suitable freedom of expression and thought. This includes the right of everyone to be heard in a spirit of dialogue which preserves a legitimate diversity within the Church.

The form of judicial procedure should give the accused the right to know his accusers and also the right to a proper defense. To be complete, justice should include speed in its procedure. This is especially necessary in marriage cases.

Finally, the members of the Church should have some share in the drawing up of decisions, in accordance with the rules given by the Second Vatican Ecumenical Council and the Holy See, for instance with regard to the setting up of councils at all levels (*Justice in the World*, Part III).

Questions for Your Reflection

1. Apply these directives to the local church as you know it, distinguishing between unjust actions of one person and unjust structures. It is easy to focus on unjust actions but it is more helpful to identify the unjust structures that produce so many unjust actions.

2. What unjust structures seem to be present at the diocesan level? at the universal level?

3. Realizing that you too are Church, what can you do to change these unjust structures?

GOSPEL EVENT

"Then the mother of Zebedee's sons. came with her sons to make a request of Jesus, and bowed low; and he said to her, 'What is it you want?' She said to him, 'Promise that these two sons of mine may sit one at your right hand and the other at your left in your kingdom.' 'You do not know what you are asking,' Jesus answered. 'Can you drink the cup that I am going to drink?' They replied, 'We can.' 'Very well,' he said, 'you shall drink my cup, but as for seats at my right hand and my left, these are not mine to grant; they belong to those to whom they have been allotted by my Father.'

"When the other ten heard this they were indignant with the two brothers. But Jesus called them to him and said, 'You know that among the pagans the rulers lord it

118

over them, and their great men make their authority felt. This is not to happen among you. No; anyone who wants to be great among you must be your servant, and anyone who wants to be first among you must be your slave, just as the Son of Man came not to be served but to serve, and to give his life as a ransom for many' " (Matthew 20:20–23).

Questions for Your Reflection

1. Contrast Jesus' idea of greatness with the world's concept of greatness. How do you feel about these two pathways to greatness?

2. Some assert that the Roman Catholic clergy's characteristic sins are ambition and envy. In the light of the Gospel story above and of your own experience, can you comment on this assertion?

3. What style of leadership does Christ expect from the leaders of his Church today?

4. What qualities would you expect to find in someone who exercises leadership in a Christ-like way?

A WORD OF CHRISTIAN WITNESS

Throughout the history of the Church various images have been used to clarify the relationship of Christ with his Church. The Church has been called a sheepfold with Christ as the Good Shepherd who lays down his life for his sheep. Often the Church has been compared to a temple or the house of God, a place where God is worshiped. It is also seen as the new Jerusalem, the center of the new covenant established by Christ between God and human beings. Paul refers to the Church as the bride of Christ for whom "he loved and delivered himself up . . . that he might sanctify her" (Ephesians 5:29). Sometimes the image of mother is used to express the life-giving and nurturing function of the Church. All of these and similar images focus on the positive aspects of the Church, on its splendor, beauty and holiness.

Jesus saw this splendor in his bride and willingly sacrificed himself for her. The apostle Paul glimpsed this same splendor in her and both described her to his Colossians and Ephesians as well as sacrificed himself for her by undergoing scourgings, stonings, hardships, and traitorous treatment. In our day the splendor of the Church shone forth when the Holy Spirit turned the Second Vatican Council into a new Pentecost by charging the Church with new life and energies to promote the updating and reform it needed.

Vatican II in its document "Dogmatic Constitution on the Church," introduced a new image which highlighted another dimension of the Church. In calling the Church the "people of God," the Council not only affirmed all the positive qualities but also confessed that being made up of human beings the Church has its sinful side too. As Christ is trying today to cleanse the Church from these defects, which include unjust structures, he invites the people of God to join him in his work. Out of a misguided loyalty, some Christians never mention the Church's defects—at neither the local, nor diocesan, nor universal level. Psychologically it is healthy to admit frankly and promptly the many weaknesses and sins in the Church, in order to avoid explosions that may have catastrophic effects. Those who keep on enduring unjust treatment in the Church and never mention it candidly build up resentments that eventually erupt in uncontrolled anger.

The more educated Christians become, the more easily will they see the Church's defects and be pained by them. Today Christians in the United States have generally been brought up to a higher level of education than found in any other country or century in the history of the Church. American Christians, then, should expect to feel more acutely than others the pressures and pains that come from unjust structures and actions in the Church.

No human community can last long unless it develops some institutional structures: specific goals, order of procedure and a coordinator. Even if these institutional structures arise largely from the "grass-roots," at least some decision-making—e.g. to convoke a meeting, to terminate discussion for a vote, to recognize speakers in this rather than that order, etc.—must come from the initiative of the coordinator and to this extent be hierarchical. The Church then as a community of the faithful must have institutional structures and leadership, but, as Jesus so clearly told his apostles, he expects a special kind of leadership. All through his public life he showed them by his example what kind of leaders they should be. On the night before he died he enacted the lesson he wished them to learn by washing their feet and then telling them they too must wash each other's feet.

Questions for Your Reflection

1. Have you unconsciously expected the Church to be perfect? to have leaders who never make mistakes? If so, what led you to such idealistic expectations?

2. What do you think of when you hear the words "the Church"? How can a focus on the universal Church be an escape from caring for the local church?

3. When you hear that a local church council has been discontinued, do you feel that this is a step forward or a step backward? Suppose your own parish council was discontinued, what concrete steps would you take as an individual? What action would you be willing to take as a member of a group?

A TWENTIETH CENTURY WITNESS

Born in 1917 of Salvadoran peasant stock, Oscar Romero became the parish priest of San Miguel, El Salvador, then a bishop in 1970, and finally the archbishop of San Salvador in 1976. When he became archbishop, he was regarded as a traditional conservative, acceptable to the wealthy oligarchy. But during his four years as archbishop the reality of his Church being persecuted changed him into a totally dedicated centrist Christian. He grew more opposed to the violence of both left and right and more committed to serve the millions of his oppressed Salvadoran people. To carry out this preferential option for the poor he faithfully followed the guidelines of Vatican II and of the later Latin American church conferences at Medellín and Puebla. But ever since the government passed a mild land-reform bill in 1975, El Salvador's powerfully rich fourteen families increasingly used all their power, including violence, to oppose its implementation. So they increasingly attacked any Church people, especially an archbishop, who supported the rights of the oppressed peasants.

Step by step, Romero experienced the persecution launched against his Church, once loyal to the status quo but now gradually becoming loyal to the integral development of *all* the Salvadorans. He had hardly begun his archdiocesan office when he found the government expelling more of his missionary priests than before, often after torturing them. At midnight on February 28, 1977, in San Salvador's cathedral plaza, government soldiers opened fire upon two thousand people gathered to protest a fraudulent election. Fifty people were killed that night, some while trying to crawl into the cathedral for refuge. On March 12, 1977, in the cane fields of Aquilares, henchmen with military-issue guns mowed down Romero's friend, Jesuit Fr. Rutilio Grande and his two companions. Further experiences like these convinced Romero how seriously El Salvador's triple power-structure—the wealthy oligarchy, the military careerists, and the traditionally conservative churchmen—formed a tripod of ruthless power that kept the peasants pinned down so the elite could cling to their privileges. Their repression fed the growing guerilla movement. In this situation, Romero's perilous job was to walk the non-violent tightrope between these two extremes. Soon in their newspapers and broadcasts the three right-wing groups coordinated their attacks against "the communist archbishop," as they labeled him.

Archbishop Romero also suffered from unjust tactics and structures from within the Salvadoran church. Earlier he had befriended a Mexican priest, Fr. Evaristo, who now betrayed him to the papal nuncio by libeling Romero as a "communist dupe." Of Romero's active fellow bishops, only Rivera y Damas consistently supported him. The others all opposed him. They often undermined his initiatives, opposed his activities or warned Rome about him. Salvador's dreadfully divided conference of bishops at first tried to show a veneer of unity. But its president, Bishop Aparicio, blamed deteriorating Church-state relations on Romero. Papal nuncio Gerada called Romero irresponsible, imprudent and inconsistent in his actions.

When Romero went to Rome, he found that negative reports had preceded him. Highhandedly Cardinal Baggio had had an apostolic visitor sent to investigate San Salvador's archbishop. This visitor had recommended that, although Romero could keep his title of archbishop, a papal delegate should be appointed to actively administer the archdiocese. Had this advice been followed, the Salvadoran church would have been even more deeply divided. Romero found that curial officials in Rome kept postponing his appointment with John Paul II. After entrusting this trouble to God's care, Romero wrote in his diary: "I even fear they may not give me the appointment. . . . In spite of everything, I love God's holy Church and will always be faithful, with his grace, to the Holy See. . . . I understand the human, the limited, the defective part of his holy Church. It remains the instrument of salvation for humanity, and I will serve it without reserve."

This dedication to the Church deepened with the months. Through his pastoral visits and especially his Sunday radio homilies, Romero became the Salvadorans' beloved shepherd. They knew his love for them, his demands for justice to all, his rejection of any violence. They felt him directing all his energies to promote among his persecuted people that divinely-given love which is the bond of unity. This courageous stand, in the face of an increasingly hostile national security state, led to many death threats and, on March 24, 1980, to his assassination at the altar while offering the Eucharist.

A few years later, an American bishop, Lawrence Welsh of Spokane, was visiting his diocesan mission in Guatemala. One night while in bed, he was suddenly awakened. Gun-slinging soldiers were standing over him. They demanded that he tell them right away where his U.S. missioners in Guatemala were hiding the (non-existent!) guns and money for the guerrillas. This rough treatment jarred Bishop Welsh into recognizing what it means to survive daily amid such violence and terror, what life in a persecuted Church is *really* like. Somehow bishops like Oscar Romero seemed the real giants in the Church, and all the unfair situations back home in Bishop Welsh's diocese, serious as some were, looked very, very small when compared with the problems of the Church in Central America.

Questions for Your Reflection

1. Does the in-fighting and maneuvering of many Salvadoran bishops and priests, all of whom say they're united through their faith in Christ, shock you? If so, how can you develop Oscar Romero's attitude as he faced the "human, the limited, the defective part" in all members of Christ's Church?

2. How did Archbishop Romero react to the opposition he experienced from other Church leaders? What evidence do you see that he became more committed to Christ, to the Church and to the poor?

3. What challenge do you experience as you reflect on Archbishop Romero and his more than 40,000 fellow Salvadorans slain in the struggle for basic human justice? How will you respond to this challenge?

4. What kind of choices are necessary to bring greater justice to your local church?

5. What kind of group meetings and activities do you think are realistically called for if you are effectively to counter unjust structures in the larger Church?

CALL TO ACTION

1. Discuss with a friend your expectations for justice, peace and harmony in the Church. What steps can you take to make your expectations more realistic?

2. Realize the great number of letters which the far right and far left mail to higher Church authorities in support of their own views. Then write at least one letter to your pastor or bishop. Congratulate him for the steps he's taking to promote Vatican II reforms in your parish or diocese. Support him by offering any service you know yourself suited to perform.

3. Be willing to pay the price of loving the Church by preparing well for meetings of local church councils or committees. Contribute your best, both during these meetings and in the follow-up work.

4. Invite several priests and several laity to an informal luncheon for discussion of ways to assess and remedy one unjust structure in your parish or diocese. In your letter of invitation, with a copy to the bishop, you might want to call their attention to the common purpose uniting all of you: to work together toward further carrying out the reforms of Vatican II and the directives of bishops as found, for example, in their 1971 Synod on Justice in the World. You might, for instance, choose to focus on this Synod's directive: "We also urge that women should have their own share of responsibility and participation in the community life of society and likewise of the Church." This might be a fruitful topic to explore in your luncheon dialogue of laity and priests.

11. Julio

Born in the 1970's, Julio is twelve years old. He grew up in Recife in northeast Brazil. When work and food gave out there, his father took the mother and their seven kids down to Sao Paulo, the industrial heart of Brazil, looking for a job. Now they live there in a slum, less than a quarter mile from the high-rise luxury hotels that line the beach. Julio has had no formal schooling but has already picked up several odd jobs. They add a bit to the meager $3.50 per day which his father earns on his job. With his youngest sister, Rosita, Julio scavenges for food in trash cans and the city dumps, just like the other children in the slums. Back in Recife, before they moved, they at least had the nourishment of black beans. Now that the government has turned thousands of acres into soybeans and other export crops, Julio's family can't even get black beans, so Rosita is severely malnourished.

Julio needs no one to tell him that here in Sao Paulo the rich are getting richer and the poor getting poorer. He may not be able to state that Brazil's top executives make more money than do their American counterparts, thanks to Brazil's so-called "economic miracle." Nor can Julio yet understand what an unemployment rate of 47% and an illiteracy rate of 67% mean in the lives of people. But from the armored jeeps of the Guardia Nacional that race through the dusty alleys of his slum, Julio clearly knows who's boss. He has seen sad-faced mothers carrying photos of a disappeared husband or son. He has also heard stories of how Brazilian soldiers imprison and torture anyone who dares resist them. Julio cannot point behind this "security" presence to the U.S. Southern Command in Panama or farther to Fort Benning and West Point as the centers of military training where the officers of these National Guardsmen learned their repressive tactics. He has seen the results of their training in the strategic use of informers, intelligence files, intimidation, disappearances, and a wide gamut of torture tactics.

If he survives, Julio will later learn that all this military training for counterinsurgency is indispensable when people with power want a national security state. He will also learn that those certain people are the wealthiest 2% of Brazil's population. They are the officers of major U.S. banks and other business corporations who require safe zones for their investments. It is this demand, Julio will discover, that shapes America's foreign policy turning developing nations of the so-called free-world into security states imprisoned by their own police and military. This U.S. policy doesn't aim to promote the mutual welfare of both peoples. Instead it seeks above all to protect and promote the political-economic interests of the U.S., regardless of what happens to little folk like Julio and Rosita.

Julio can already see in his own bone-thin body (5′3″ and 87 lbs.) the effects of this policy. If Brazil's government needs the biggest army and police force in Latin America to keep the peasants quiet it must have a huge defense budget. This priority robs the millions of Brazil's poor people of their God-given right to use Brazil's natural resources for their own integral human development.

The story of Julio and his sister is symbolic of thousands of other undernourished, illiterate, Brazilian children. Their pictures have appeared in newspapers and on TV screens around the world. Seeing these two tragedies,

America's allies in Europe, Canada, Japan and Australia increasingly oppose this U.S. foreign policy. They see that it violates basic human rights, pushes millions of people to sympathize with communism, and alienates allies America needs.

Questions for Your Reflection

1. As you read this case, did you tend to think "sob story"? If so, what has influenced you to think this way?

2. There are millions of children in Brazil living like Julio. What unjust structures keep these children in such poverty?

3. On reading about Julio, did you think that over-population was a main cause of his tragedy? If so, can you detect what influences have made you tend to think so?

4. In imagination, walk through your ordinary day with Julio at your side. Try to discover the services and things you take for granted but which Julio has never experienced.

5. Which persons benefit most from Brazil's so-called "economic miracle"? Which structures keep Brazil's overall population from benefitting by it?

6. You hear that Brazil's Catholic bishops have charted a new course for the Church there by "taking a preferential option for the poor." What meaning does that news have for you? How is that option touching the lives of many of Brazil's Julios?

An Experiment

(*Caution:* This experiment is not intended to evoke guilt feelings since most of the guilt belongs to the unjust systems that link Latinos with you. Rather the experiment aims to alert you to the real people at the other end of our simplest habits and to those very complex politico-economic systems which connect our lives with theirs.)

Suppose that at breakfast this morning you had a cup of coffee and some cereal covered with banana slices. Suppose, too, that you put a bit of sugar in your coffee and on your cereal. Try to trace back that coffee, banana and sugar to their roots in the soil.

First, do you find that migrant worker, perhaps a relative of Julio's, who picked those coffee beans that went into your cup of coffee? Does he look as malnourished, even if older and more weatherbeaten than Julio?

Next, do you recognize that Guatemalan Indian woman, with sharp Mayan features that crown her beautifully woven tribal costume? Isn't she the one who wrapped and sealed in a plastic bag that banana stalk from which came those slices on your cereal? She's too illiterate to read warnings but she's not immune to a tarantula in a banana bunch or to the herbicide dust in the sweatshop where she packages those bananas.

And your sugar—wasn't it first harvested by that fifteen year old Honduran lad whose machete sliced the cane from which your sweetening crystals finally came? Although the Honduran sun can broil this boy's body, he doesn't even get $3.50 a day for his cane-cutting.

Questions for Your Reflection

1. If coffee is the single largest commodity in international trade, apart from petroleum, why aren't the coffee producing countries among the richest in the world?

2. Brazil, Colombia, Ecuador, El Salvador, and Guatemala depend on their coffee crop for 17% to 52% of the money they use to purchase U.S. imports. What happens to these countries' largely one-crop economies if the price of unroasted coffee beans suddenly drops by 20%?

3. The U.S. coffee industry imports bags of un-

roasted coffee from Latin America. This unroasted coffee is then processed, packaged, distributed and sold by the U.S. coffee industry. The industry generates about 175,000 jobs for U.S. workers and about one billion dollars in wages. What right have we Americans unilaterally to require that coffee grown in Latin America cannot be processed there, but only in the United States? (Derived from Thomas Fenton, *Education for Justice,* Maryknoll, N.Y.: Orbis, 1975, p. 308.)

4. What do you predict would happen if native Guatemalan peasant women tried to organize into a union?

5. What does the huge U.S. military build-up in Honduras really mean as regards our American stand toward Central American countries? What will it mean to the machete-swinging lad who started your breakfast sugar on its way to you?

GOSPEL EVENT

"When Pentecost day came round, they [the apostles, the mother of Jesus, some other women and brethren] had all met in one room, when suddenly they heard what sounded like a powerful wind from heaven, the noise of which filled the entire house in which they were sitting; and something appeared to them that seemed like tongues of fire; these separated and came to rest on the head of each of them. They were all filled with the Holy Spirit, and began to speak foreign languages as the Spirit gave them the gift of speech.

"Now there were devout men living in Jerusalem from every nation under heaven, and at this sound they all assembled, each one bewildered to hear these men speaking his own language. They were amazed and astonished. 'Surely,' they said, 'all these men speaking are Galileans? How does it happen that each of us hears them in his own native language? Parthians, Medes and Elamites; people from Mesopotamia, Judaea and Cappadocia, Pontus and Asia, Phrygia and Pamphilia, Egypt and the parts of Libya round Cyrene; as well as visitors from Rome—Jews and proselytes alike—Cretans and Arabs; we hear them preaching in our own language about the marvels of God.' Everyone was amazed and unable to explain it; they asked one another what it all meant" (Acts 2:1–12).

Questions for Your Reflection

1. Is Pentecost a finished event or is it somehow going on today? If it is going on today, what evidence do you see that the Spirit is calling people of all kinds into unity?

2. What influences are at work in the world to separate people, to cause disunity?

3. Can any member of a rich nation promote justice among nations if he or she lacks reverence for all persons? Explain your answer.

4. In today's world do you see the one reality of basic human needs working to unite north and south, east and west? Give evidence for your answer.

5. To satisfy their basic human need for subsistence and growth, the diverse peoples who assembled at Pentecost all depended ecologically on each one's tribal land and resources, with trade being secondary to subsistence. Do trade agreements today look primarily to letting the land and resources of each country be that people's God-given source of sustenance and growth? Is there injustice involved in these trade agreements? Explain.

A WORD OF CHRISTIAN WITNESS

Today some people insist that our east-west relationship is America's #1 trouble-spot. Other voices insist that increasingly it is our north-south relationship that causes the greatest problems. Rather, it is necessary to see the living reality that unites both relationships.

Basically just relations with aggressive communist regimes can be achieved. There is a need to place more emphasis on basic human needs common to both groups. Both communists and Americans want to survive—no small feat in this nuclear age! People of both countries want peace, want basic respect and tolerance from the other, want to gradually raise the standard of living for their own people. These desires will never be achieved as long as the ordinary people are robbed and the economic systems destroyed by the continuing build-up of arms. Instead of challenging each other to unneeded and foolhardy increases in military, especially nuclear, defense, both east and west can change their emphases. Both can emphasize the better gathering of intelligence so that prompter effective sanctions can be applied. Instead of threats of military retaliation, diplomatic negotiations, economic sanctions and moral influence with other nations are possibilities for solving differences. To small nations occupied by a super-power through clearly unjust tactics, the other super-power can offer limited support of covert activities to counter that injustice. All intercultural and economic exchanges that build up mutual knowledge, defuse suspicious, and increase trust should be fostered wherever possible.

To achieve basically just relations with third world countries in Latin America, the U.S. must be shaken out of its materialistic frame of mind into a mind-set that focuses mostly on human persons to be developed. This change of focus should lead to a change of practice by

American banks and transnational corporations who today concentrate on making a profit without regard for the
cultural and ethnic richness of the third world country.
The security and profit of the dominant nation is the first
consideration in setting up international politico-economic structures and policies rather than the basic human needs of the people. At present, U.S. corporations are
so over-concerned with increasing production and con-
sumption that they cannot hear the cry of the poor of the
south, the cry of millions of starving children, the cry of
refugees and war-torn families, the cry of disinherited
and unemployed peasants. Our policy of setting up national security states only further tightens the lid on an
already boiling pot and drives the desperate and starving
peoples toward the communists.

Actually this cry from the south can save the U.S. if
it is heard and acted upon. A more just response to the
south would create ways to meet not only people's emergency needs, but especially their regular needs for basic
foods, medicines, education, labor-intensive industries,
and for all that is necessary for integral human development. Latin America, Africa and other parts of the third
world offer an economic market, which, if not distorted by
greed and military suppression, can save the economic
machine of the U.S.

Questions for Your Reflection

1. Do you believe that it is possible to achieve just relations with communist nations, especially Russia? Support your answer with some basic facts.
2. How can ordinary people in both east and west
help to bring about better relations between nations?
3. How do you think our relations with Latin Amer-

ica could be improved? What contribution can you make to bettering these relations?

A TWENTIETH CENTURY WITNESS

Mohandas Gandhi grew up as a boy under British rule in the city of Porbandar in the Gujarat province of western India. As chief minister of the city, his father knew how to steer a way between tough British political officers, unpredictable Indian princes and the long-suffering people. Mohandas would develop this skill to the full. His mother, a devout Hindu with a tinge of Jainism, prayed, fasted and often wore herself out caring for her family's sick ones. Thus she strongly influenced Mohandas. His vegetarianism, care for the suffering, prayerfulness, tolerance of people of different creeds, and attitude of non-injury to any living thing derived from his early training that he kept reinforcing by his prayerfulness.

After a lawyer's education in London University, Mohandas was hired for one year by an Indian firm as its representative in South Africa. Journeying from Durban to Pretoria, he was thrown out of a first class railway compartment and left shivering at the depot at Pietermaritzburg. Not long after, he was beaten up for not making room for European passengers. Through these experiences Gandhi came to his moment of truth. He understood how oppressed were his Indian people there and how much in need of a lawyer's defense. He spent more than twenty years in South Africa defending his people and forming the Indian Congress Party there.

In 1914 he returned to India where through more than three decades he became the non-violent leader of his people to independence from the British yoke. Imprisoned at least three times, he provided outstanding leadership in three different periods. Called a mahatma (great-souled one), he chiefly taught non-possessiveness and the ability to remain unruffled by pains or pleasures. When the British murderously fired into a group of four hundred innocent Indian women, men and children, killing them all, Gandhi came to see how insensitive the British were to Indians' feelings. He recognized that only the disciplined use of firmness in truth could eventually break through the calloused consciences of these colonizing capitalists. He knew it would take the bruised bodies and bloodied brows of many of his non-violent resisters to teach the British to become human toward other races. He felt it was a price worth paying. Through those three decades of marching, confronting, fasting and weaving, pleading with arguing Moslems and Hindus, even to the point of being assassinated by a Hindu fanatic, Gandhi paid the price.

Why then is Gandhi such a leader and symbol for healing unjust international structures? His religiously-based non-violent movement succeeded in overturning the unjust structures of colonialism, racism, and materialistic capitalism. If the British turned India into a security state by their bobbies and guns, he had a different but mightier weapon: truth firmly witnessed, without violence, on religious grounds. For his response to the unjust structures of his time was basically religious, drawn from the Hindu scripture, the *Bhagavadgita*. He explained that for him religion did not mean sectarianism, dogma, formalism or ritual. Rather, he said in his autobiography, "What I have been striving and pining to achieve these thirty years is to see God face to face." His contemplative prayer did not take him to a mountain hermitage apart, but he found God in the faces of the poor or powerful he dealt with and in the weaving and walking he did. He had met Christianity in London during his studies there, and when asked what he thought of Christ, Gandhi replied, "Oh, Christ is a most admirable leader.

But I cannot admire most Christians since they do not really follow him."

He challenged materialistic capitalism with his religiously-based truth-force. His example of weaving and his stress on cottage industries taught Indians to resist the lure of the cities and their ever bigger factories. In this way he fostered domestic industries in the villages and helped free Indians from depending on the mills of Manchester for textiles.

When he eventually resigned from the Indian Congress Party's leadership, it was only in order to concentrate on building up the Indian nation from the bottom. In 1942, having arrived at the point where they could assume home rule, he stood up to the British and told them to withdraw immediately from his people's soil, for the British were trespassing.

His chief regret in the end was that he was unable to prevent various religious factions and the British from dividing India along religious lines. The creation of Pakistan and India occasioned the mutual killing of thousands of Hindus and Moslems. One of Gandhi's last works was to attempt reconciliation of these factions.

In brief, then, in a time of deepening crisis in north-south relations, of social apathy in the affluent societies, of the shadow of unbridled technology and a most precarious peace threatened by nuclear terror, it seems likely that Mahatma Gandhi's life, example, ideas, and techniques will become increasingly relevant.

Questions for Your Reflection

1. How did Gandhi's earlier life prepare him for his type of leadership among his people?

2. Gandhi believed that the only way to conquer violence is by non-violent resistance. Do you believe that this is a Christian stand toward violence?

3. Is it possible for truth-force in non-violent resistance to change unjust structures? Give some examples.
4. Are there any non-violent movements in the U.S. that are attempting to change unjust structures? What effect are they having?
5. Comment on Gandhi's statement that Christians do not follow the teachings of Christ. Do you think there is any truth to this statement today in the U.S.?

CALL TO ACTION

1. Can you, as an individual or as a group, join a nationally-researched movement that aims to remedy unjust international structures (e.g., Bread for the World, to counter widespread starvation and malnutrition; Network, to examine Congressional bills for their bearings on North-South relationships)?

2. Examine whether Gandhi's life of religiously rooted respect for others, self-disciplined vegetarianism, and courageous non-violent insistence on the rights of his people may not provide you with a remedy in our consumeristic, materialistic American culture. Resolve to take one step to counter consumerism in your life.

12. David

When David graduated from college he wanted to do something worthwhile with his life. He wasn't sure what direction his life should take, so he decided to join the Peace Corps for three years. He was sent to Peru where he worked with the Indians, helping them to learn better ways of raising their crops.

David's experiences of helping the poor had convinced him that he should dedicate his life as a layman to working for justice when he returned to the U.S. Seeing so many young men turning to drugs and alcohol because they were unable to find work, David opened a halfway house. There those who wanted to be free of their addictions could begin a new life. The young men coming to the rehabilitation center were put on a strict schedule of work, group therapy, individual counseling and study. They were expected to help on the farm associated with the center, attend the group sessions and cooperate with the counselor. Each young man was given the opportunity to develop some job skills and the staff did its best to help each one find suitable employment.

One man who came to the center for help was Carl. He had been in the hospital for several weeks in a detoxification program. His doctor had frightened Carl when he warned him that his days were numbered unless he stopped drinking completely. Every time he had a drink he could not stop until he passed out. Sometimes several days would go by without Carl knowing what he was doing or where he was. Now Carl decided he had better do something about his problem, so he checked himself into the rehabilitation center.

After several months at the center Carl seemed ready and eager to take complete responsibility for his own life. With the help of his counselor he found a job selling insurance. For several months he worked hard and seemed to be getting along with the other employees. He and a fellow-worker, Jack, became good friends.

One Friday after Jack and Carl had received their pay checks Jack talked Carl into going to a bar for "just one drink." As Carl drank with Jack, he began to get angry at David for depriving him of having fun drinking with his friends. The more he drank the more angry he became.

When Carl finally left the bar at 2:00 A.M. he went to the rehabilitation center, dumped several trash cans on the front porch and set the trash on fire. Fortunately, all the residents got out the back door safely, but extensive damage was done to the house. David was furious. "After all I did for him, that low-down drunk! I'll never forgive him for this!" Carl tried to tell David that he was sorry, but David would not even listen to him. Soon afterward, David left the center and took a job selling computers. "I'm through trying to help people—they're not worth it," he said.

Questions for Your Reflection

1. Do you feel that David was sincere in his work for justice? Give evidence for your answer.
2. What seemed to motivate David in starting the rehabilitation center?
3. Would you call David a just person? Why or why not?

4. How do you think David should respond to Carl's ingratitude? To Carl's expression of sorrow?

5. If you were in David's place what would you do in this situation?

Experiment

1. Interview someone who is operating a rehabilitation center or a free store. As you talk with this person try to sense how this individual handles ingratitude, anger or even violence from those he or she is trying to help.

2. During the week check your newspaper carefully for any articles or reports that are examples of forgiveness or unforgiveness. How do you react to these incidents?

GOSPEL EVENT

"One of the Pharisees invited Jesus to a meal. When he arrived at the Pharisee's house and took his place at table, a woman came in who had a bad name in the town. She had heard he was dining with the Pharisee and had brought with her an alabaster jar of ointment. She waited behind him at his feet, weeping, and her tears fell on his feet, and she wiped them away with her hair; then she covered his feet with kisses and anointed them with the ointment.

"When the Pharisee who had invited him saw this, he said to himself, 'If this man were a prophet, he would know who this woman is that is touching him and what a bad name she has.' Then Jesus took him up and said, 'Simon, I have something to say to you.' 'Speak, Master,' was the reply. 'There was once a creditor who had two men in his debt; one owed him five hundred denarii, the other fifty. They were unable to pay, so he pardoned them both. Which of them will love him more?' 'The one who was pardoned more, I suppose,' answered Simon. Jesus said, 'You are right.'

"Then he turned to the woman. 'Simon,' he said, 'you see this woman? I came into your house, and you poured no water over my feet, but she has poured out her tears over my feet and wiped them away with her hair. You gave me no kiss, but she has been covering my feet with kisses ever since I came in. You did not anoint my head with oil, but she has anointed my feet with ointment. For this reason I tell you that her sins, her many sins, must have been forgiven her, or she would not have shown such great love. It is the man who is forgiven little who shows little love. Then he said to her, 'Your sins are forgiven.' Those who were with him at table began to say to themselves, 'Who is this man, that he even forgives sins?' But he said to the woman, 'Your faith has saved you; go in peace' " (Luke 7:36–50).

Questions for Your Reflection

1. How does Jesus react to the discourtesy of Simon?

2. What is the relationship between forgiveness and love that Jesus points out in this incident? In light of this relationship, how do you explain Jesus' comment to the woman, "Your faith has saved you"?

3. Have you had the experience of being forgiven by another person and then realizing that you now love that person more?

4. Does this connection between forgiveness and love apply to our relationship with God also? Why or why not?

A WORD OF CHRISTIAN WITNESS

As David works hard to overcome the injustices around him he is in good company. As long ago as the time of Job, people who sought a closer relationship with God realized the importance of working for justice. Job's description of himself might well be applied to justice advocates today. Job says: "I had dressed myself in righteousness like a garment; justice, for me, was a cloak and turban. I was eyes for the blind, and feet for the lame. Who but I was father of the poor? The stranger's case had a hearing from me. I used to break the fangs of wicked men, and snatch their prey from between their jaws" (Job 29:14–17).

Micah, too, points out the human effort that is needed in becoming just when he says: "This is what Yahweh asks of you: only this, to act justly, to love tenderly and to walk humbly with your God" (Micah 6:8).

Anyone who tries to follow the example of Job and the instructions of Micah soon reaches a crisis point as David did. It becomes clear that no matter how hard one tries, even in the company of a loving supporting community, human efforts are not enough to bring about the liberation of the human spirit. Oppressive structures can be attacked and changed for greater justice to the poor, the marginated, and those who cannot help themselves. But in the last analysis, both oppressor and oppressed are still not free and at peace until they receive liberation from God. This may be a hard lesson to learn in a world where technology, psychology, and sociology all provide greater know-how to get things done. A person can become self-sufficient and forget that it is God who justifies and keeps calling and drawing us to greater justification.

Hebrew history shows that the Israelites were very aware of the paradox that they must work for justice, but that justice is a gift from God. Isaiah writes, "Send victory like dew, you heavens, and let the clouds rain it down. Let the earth open for salvation to spring up. Let deliverance, too, bud forth which I, Yahweh, shall create" (Isaiah 45:8). (Note: As the Jerusalem Bible explains, the Hebrew word "sedeq" here rendered "victory" is usually translated "integrity," "righteousness," "justice"; so also "sedaqah," "deliverance" at the end of the verse.)

As this verse from Isaiah indicates, the biblical understanding of justice is much broader and deeper than the concept of justice held by most Americans. A just or righteous person in the biblical sense is an individual of God-given integrity, one who has a right relationship with God, self and others.

In writing to the Romans, Paul echoes the thought of Isaiah but adds several other dimensions. He points out, first of all, that because of sin, a spiritual deadness pervaded human existence. There was no antidote for this spiritual death, but Jesus came bringing forgiveness from the Father. This forgiveness is a free gift, bestowing life and righteousness on those who receive it. This righteousness makes it possible to lovingly serve all those whom God loves. In Paul's words, "If it is certain that death reigned over everyone as the consequence of one man's fall, it is even more certain that one man, Jesus Christ, will cause everyone to reign in life who receives the free gift that he does not deserve, of being made righteous." In order that the close link between forgiveness and justice will not be missed Paul continues to press his point: "Again, as one man's fall brought condemnation on everyone, so the good act of one man brings everyone life and makes them justified" (Romans 5:17–18).

Looking at the case of David, it seems that he has failed to realize that the justice of God is poured out on sinful, weak humanity, not in wrath and punishment, but in forgiveness. To take part in this justice of God, to become a just person, necessarily involves taking part in God's operation of extending forgiveness to all who open themselves to it. It involves a willingness to accept God's loving forgiveness, the redemptive graces of Jesus. God's justice is expressed in this loving forgiveness which liberates the soul of inner oppression. A person is not free to treat others with loving forgiveness until that person has first admitted the need of God's forgiveness. Once a person has experienced forgiveness and grown to be a more just person, then that individual can work more effectively to help others to greater justice, knowing that justice work often involves forgiving.

It is not enough then to actively seek justice for oneself and others, to attempt to change unjust structures. At the same time, the justice worker must desire to become a just person. Becoming just does not depend so much on the individual's efforts as on the heartfelt desire that is a prayer to receive God's gift. It is God who justifies. This then is the paradox. Justice is a gift of God but somehow it also depends on the efforts of human beings.

Beyond this paradox is a dynamic at work which is basic to all of Christian life. It is God who always takes the initiative. He gifts the individual with faith, love, hope, justice and forgiveness. Because the person has been so gifted, he or she can then respond faithfully to God, can love God, self and others, can struggle for justice and forgive from a loving heart. The fact that one has been so gifted does not mean that the response is automatic or even easy. God's gifts do not eliminate human weakness, resistance, or sinfulness that inhibits the wholehearted response. But when God finds an open heart he is not only present in his gifts but he is also at work in these gifts. He works in and through the human person so that his gifts become productive.

If David had realized that he was not alone in struggling for justice he would have asked God to work justice in him to make him a just person. As David viewed the damage caused by Carl, he needed to turn to God, first asking to be forgiven for any harm he had caused to others. Only then would he be free enough to respond to what God wanted to do in and through him, to forgive Carl.

David's justice would then image the justice of God, for from it would flow forgiveness.

What this means is that we are called to be the freely cooperating instruments of God's mercy toward all of us human sinners. His compassion for all of us, caught in the injustice of sin and sinful habits, is the compassion we need to employ toward ourselves and toward both oppressors and oppressed, as God does. By listening to Christ's continuing call to acknowledge our sinfulness and our need of God's forgiveness and mercy, we are led to broadcast Christ's fundamental message: "The time has come and the kingdom of God is close at hand. Repent and believe the good news" (Mark 1:15).

Questions for Your Reflection

1. What did Job mean when he said, "Justice for me was cloak and turban"?

2. Describe a person who follows Micah's instruction "to act justly, to love tenderly, and to walk humbly." In what way is this a description of the Christian life? Can you mention some aspects of the Christian life not included in Micah's statement?

3. How have you experienced the paradox that justice is a gift of God but it also depends on you?

4. In what ways have you experienced God's love, justice and forgiveness working through you? What was the result of this union of your activity with God's?

A TWENTIETH CENTURY WITNESS

Perhaps the most crucial test of Martin Luther King, Jr.'s God-like universal love came when he encountered treason. Jesus had kept loving Judas even after the kiss of the traitor. Could King?

King's testing came during the Montgomery boycott. Rev. U.J. Fields, one of King's most trusted assistants, had attacked the entire non-violent movement. Fields told the press that he resigned as the recording secretary of the Montgomery Improvement Association. He charged that members of the association were misusing funds and were lining their own pockets with donations intended for the boycott. Moreover, Fields claimed that the leaders of the movement clearly wanted to perpetuate themselves in office. All these false charges against the movement had been hurled earlier by King's white opponents. But now these charges stung much more, coming from a friend King relied upon.

Gradually the reason for Fields' behavior came to light. The executive board of the association had decided not to continue him in office and Fields was taking out his anger on the association and at the same time hurting his friend, King. Fields' revenge, however, backfired. His own congregation rejected him, as did the whole black community. Filled with regret and shame, Fields soon met with King. Fields admitted that he knew there was no misuse of funds. He confessed that his only motive in all this was to get even with the executive board.

Fields had inflicted a deep wound on the association and on King. He had smeared the leaders of the association and had endangered the flow of gifts essential for maintaining the boycott. Yet, like the forgiving father in Jesus' parable, King reached out to Fields to forgive and restore this brother who had strayed. In doing so King was counting on the only energy strong enough to embrace the traitor, God's own forgiving love.

However, King went beyond his own personal forgiveness. He helped Fields return to the good graces of the black community. In the face of an offended and angry audience, King introduced Fields by reminding them how every human being is frail. Hadn't Jesus told the story of the prodigal son so his followers could imitate the forgiving father rather than the unforgiving elder son? So moved was the audience by King's loving forgiveness which they recognized as authentic that they accepted Fields' retraction and apology with applause. King's nonviolent forgiving love had vindicated itself. It had turned a ruinous threat to the association into something that unified it more than ever.

Questions for Your Reflection

1. Which do you find more difficult—to become a just person or to work for justice for others? Give the basis for your answer.

2. Think of three events in your life when you found it difficult to forgive someone who had hurt you. Try to get in touch with the motives that moved you to forgive in spite of the resistance you felt.

3. Is there anyone you have not been able to forgive? What is blocking you from forgiving this person? Do you feel that you are justified in refusing forgiveness to this person? Why or why not?

4. Do you think it is possible to forgive someone but not be able to forget the injustice you suffered? How do you distinguish between forgiving and forgetting an injury?

CALL TO ACTION

1. Spend some time paging through this book slowly and reflectively, reviewing the insights you have had, the things you have learned from the group, the actions you have decided to take. From this review decide on one thing you will do that will help to make you a more just

person and a course of action that will bring greater justice to others.

2. Decide how you will encourage and support one another in your efforts for justice.

3. Plan a way in which the group will ritualize or symbolize these decisions for justice.